RESTRICTIVE BUSINESS PRACTICES OF MULTINATIONAL ENTERPRISES:

Report of the Committee of Experts on Restrictive Business Practices

The decision to publish this report was taken in July 1977

ORGANISATION FOR ECONOMIC CO-OPERATION AND DEVELOPMENT,

Committee of Experts on Restrictive Business Practices,

The Organisation for Economic Co-operation and Development (OECD) was set up under a Convention signed in Paris on 14th December, 1960, which provides that the OECD shall promote policies designed:

- to achieve the highest sustainable economic growth and employment and a rising standard of living in Member countries, while maintaining financial stability, and thus to contribute to the development of the world economy;
- to contribute to sound economic expansion in Member as well as non-member countries in the process of economic development;
- to contribute to the expansion of world trade on a multilateral, non-discriminatory basis in accordance with international obligations.

The Members of OECD are Australia, Austria, Belgium, Canada, Denmark, Finland, France, the Federal Republic of Germany, Greece, Iceland, Ireland, Italy, Japan, Luxembourg, the Netherlands, New Zealand, Norway, Portugal, Spain, Sweden, Switzerland, Turkey, the United Kingdom and the United States.

* *
*

TABLE OF CONTENTS

Chapter one

ECONOMIC AND EMPIRICAL ANALYSIS OF THE EFFECTS
OF MULTINATIONAL ENTERPRISES ON COMPETITION

Chapter two

POSSIBILITES OF APPLYING RESTRICTIVE
BUSINESS PRACTICES LEGISLATION
TO THE ACTIVITIES OF MULTINATIONAL ENTERPRISES

Chapter three

POSSIBLE REMEDIES AND SUGGESTIONS
FOR ACTION

ANNEXES

FOREWORD

Multinational enterprises have become an important factor in the world economy, principally because of their frequently large size and their international character. As a group, they probably accounted for 20 per cent of world GNP in 1971, excluding the centrally planned economies. More than 200 of them have annual gross sales exceeding one billion dollars each and affiliates in twenty or more countries[1]*. They have been a major vehicle for investment in both developed and developing countries. Because of these factors, multinational enterprises have had an important impact on competition both in international commerce and in national markets and have raised serious issues with regard to competition policy and procedures within the OECD Member nations and elsewhere.

The OECD Committee of Experts on Restrictive Business Practices has been studying the problems raised by the restrictive business practices of multinational enterprises for several years. In 1969, a recommendation was made at the Cambridge International Conference on Monopolies, Mergers and Restrictive Practices sponsored by the OECD that the Committee should consider this question and was one of the factors prompting the Committee to undertake a study of the restrictive business practices of multinational enterprises. This work was started by the Committee in 1970. In 1972, the problems raised by multinational enterprises were stressed in the OECD report on " Policy Perspectives for International Trade and Economic Relations" (the Rey report) which was the starting point for the overall studies on multinational enterprises undertaken since by the Organisation. In 1974 the Committee was instructed by the OECD Council to focus upon the problems raised for competition policy by the activities of related firms belonging to the same multinational enterprises as regards, in particular, such questions as the geographical division of markets, the exchange of goods and services between related enterprises and the use of patents and licences. The Committee was also invited to contribute to the drafting of guidelines for multinational enterprises relating to competition which were ultimately incorporated in the guidelines promulgated on 21st June, 1976 by the OECD Council at Ministerial level (see Annex IV).

The present report by the Committee is based on extensive factual evidence and competition enforcement experience provided by 19 Member countries and by the Commission of the European Communities. It was decided that the report would focus on what the Committee believed to be the significant issues of competition policy and procedures relating to multinational enterprises rather than attempt an overall evaluation of the economic effects of multinational enterprises or even of the overall impact on competition of multinational enterprises. The report contains three chapters. The first chapter consists of a brief introduction covering definitional problems and a short history of multinational enterprises, followed by a theoretical and empirical analysis of their extent and nature, the motives for their formation, and their pro- and anti-competitive effects. Four principal types of restrictive behaviour in which some multinational enterprises have engaged are described on the basis of cases dealt with by

---

* The notes and references will be found at the end of the report.

national administrative and judicial authorities: international allocation of production and markets, international pricing abuses, anti-competitive international mergers, and unduly restrictive international patent licensing. The second chapter is concerned with the application of national[2] restrictive business practices legislation to multinational enterprises and discusses the difficulties which have been encountered in connection with such application. The final chapter discusses a number of measures which could be taken at national and international levels to remedy the problems identified in the report.

The Committee of Experts on Restrictive Business Practices approved this report in December 1976 and the report generally reflects the situation as at that date.

Chapter One

ECONOMIC AND EMPIRICAL ANALYSIS OF THE EFFECTS OF MULTINATIONAL ENTERPRISES ON COMPETITION

I. Definition

1.   There are rather differing definitions[3] of the term "multinational enterprises" ; a generally acceptable definition has not yet been established. Most of the studies of multinationals made so far, however, use definitions based on the direct investment concept. For the purpose of the present report the Committee retained the following definition: "A multinational enterprise is an enterprise which carries out operations, such as production of goods or the provision of services, in more than one country through component units which are subject to some measure of central control".

2.   It is true that this definition and the definitions of direct investment are not identical, since direct investment can also be made by private persons and since central control of enterprises operating in several countries does not necessarily presuppose a commitment in terms of capital but may also be exercised on the basis of contractual commitments. However, as the volume of direct investment made by private parties as well as the cases of central control merely based on contractual commitment are only of minor importance, for the purpose of this report the terms "direct investment" and "multinational enterprise" are considered synonymous. The advantage of this approach is that available statistical material on direct investment can be used for an analysis of multinational enterprises.

3.   The definitions which contain additional qualitative and quantitative criteria are somewhat unsatisfactory in that they do not ensure the complete coverage of all enterprises operating on an international level which are significant for competition policy.   In particular, a definition which limits the coverage to manufacturing enterprises only would seem to be too narrow in view of the economic importance of large and internationally operating enterprises in the banking and insurance industries, in trade and commerce (other than enterprises simply engaged in exporting or importing) as well as in other service industries. In addition, the definition should also cover public and semi-public enterprises operating in more than one market since they may also pose the same problems, from the competition point of view, as purely private enterprises. The sometimes proposed quantitative criteria – such as turnover outside the home country or number of countries in which the enterprise operates – are also unsatisfactory, at least from the competition policy point of view, although the aim of this approach, viz. to exclude enterprises of less economic importance doing business abroad is, in principle, commendable.

4.   In view of these difficulties of definition, it has been suggested that a list of enterprises satisfying a number of specific criteria should be drawn up instead of using

a general definition. But this, too, involves considerable disadvantages. Apart from appearing somewhat arbitrary, and as opposed to a definition based on the direct investment concept, hardly any figures are available at present to permit such an approach, not to mention the fact that the enterprises which would appear in such a list would also account for the greater part of direct investment[4]. The disadvantages connected with a general definition based on objective criteria seem to be less significant. Nevertheless it should be recognised that much of the economic and competitive concern about multinational enterprises stems primarily from the growth and activities of the largest multinational enterprises which operate facilities in a wide range of countries and which enjoy substantial power in at least some markets.

5.   One of the most controversial aspects so far in discussions about multinational enterprises has been that of competition policy. Depending on the assumptions made or actual characteristics of this type of enterprise when assessing it in terms of competition policy, the multinational enterprise is considered either as an instrument for removing or at least reducing market imperfections affecting competition, or diametrically opposed to this, it is considered responsible for a growing transformation of a system of decentralised market control into a centralised planning systems ultimately dominated by a limited group of enterprises acting on a world-wide scale. One reason explaining the variations in competitive assessments of multinational enterprises has been the inability to identify the competitive problems stemming from their multinational character rather than from their mere size and market power. Another reason has been the slow development of systematic study of their competitive effects and practices. In the absence of sufficient knowledge of the implications of multinational enterprises for competition policy a final assessment taking into account a number of other objectives of economic policy, for example, growth, distribution, balance-of-payments and employments effects, to mention just the most important, is made more difficult.

II. History

6.   The trend towards the internationalisation of production in its broadest sense can be roughly divided into three stages: the first stage during which direct foreign investment was made on a considerable scale began approximately in the middle of the 19th century and ended with the outbreak of World War I. The second stage, marked initially by a recovery of foreign activities by private enterprises, but followed by stagnation and then an absolute decline in these activities, comprised the inter-war period. The third and not yet terminated stage in this development started at the end of World War II and has been marked by an almost steady, large-scale growth of direct investment.

7.   There is no comprehensive and detailed information as to the extent and development of direct investment during the initial stage. It is known, however, that a number of today's important multinational enterprises, particulary in the extractive and manufacturing industries, were established during this period. One of the main reasons for the growing foreign orientation during the first stage of the internationalisation process as far as manufacturing industries are concerned was the growing protectionism in foreign trade in the latter part of the 19th century, which was aimed at furthering the development of domestic industries. Due to the fact that unlike foreign trade, international capital transactions were not at that time subject to restrictions, conditions were favourable for the development of private direct investments. In 1914, British investments abroad amounted to £4.0 thousand million, German investments to £1.2 thousand million and United States investments to £600 million[5], by far the greater part of which, however, were portfolio investments[6] where considerations of yield rather than of control were in the foreground.

8. Economic developments during the inter-war period were characterised particulary by cross-frontier cartelisation covering most key areas. Except perhaps for the United States, these developments were almost unhampered by national competition laws. This seems to be due above all to the continuing concentration process which created oligopolistic market structures in at least some economically significant areas and favoured the establishment of national and international price and market allocation agreements. By contrast, the development of direct investment shows a trend in the opposite direction: direct investment declined while cartelisation increased[7]. The theoretical assumption that cartelisation has a negative effect on investments abroad is supported by the observation that the increase in direct investments during the third stage is particularly important in areas such as the chemical industry, mechanical engineering and raw material extraction, where during the second stage cartelisation was particulary widespread.

9. At the beginning of the Great Depression, the internationalisation of production reached a temporary standstill. Due to world-wide over-capacity and political developments unfavourable to the propensity to invest, foreign establishments became very rare. The overall foreign commitment even declined in absolute terms. The book value of all United States direct investments in 1946 amounted to $7.2 thousand million as against $7.5 thousand million in 1929[8].

10. The period following World War II has been characterised by the unprecedented growth of foreign investment. Initially this development was determined above all by United States direct investment which nearly trebled from 1950 to 1960 and again from 1960 to 1971, amounting to approximately $86 thousand million in 1972[9]. The Western European countries and Japan – the most important foreign investors after the United States – started later to participate in the process of internationalisation of production because priority was given to the reconstruction of domestic production capacity which had been destroyed during the war and capital transactions were subject to control up until the sixties. The extent of this development is illustrated by the growth rates of direct investment of the United States, the United Kingdom, Japan and the Federal Republic of Germany which accounted for nearly 75 per cent of all direct investments in 1971. For the period 1960-1965 the average annual percentage growth rates amounted to 27.0 for Japan, 22.3 for the Federal Republic of Germany, 7.0 for the United Kingdom and 8.5 for the United States. For the period 1965-1971 the corresponding percentages were 29.4 (Japan), 23.2 (Federal Republic of Germany), 6.1 (United Kingdom) and 9.7 (United States)[10].

11. The development of foreign production since the middle of the 19th century shows that multinational enterprises as such are not a new phenomenon. What are new, however, are the economic, social and political problems raised by these enterprises as a result of the size and character they assumed only during the third stage of development. At the turn of the century, for example, United States enterprises operated less than 100 production facilities abroad[11] as against a "minimum number of affiliates" of 9,691 in 1968-1969[12] and the total number of persons employed by United States-owned companies in the United Kingdom, the main recipient of United States investment, in 1914 was as low as 12,000[13] as against approximately 442,400 in 1963 employed in manufacturing industries alone[14]. The insignificance of the role played by multinational enterprises in earlier stages in relation to overall economic activity in the industrialised countries is also demonstrated by the fact that around 1914 all main companies in the then most important industries – coal, railways, iron and steel, engineering, shipbuilding, textiles, agriculture and agricultural products – were national[15].

12. Apart from this quantitative increase in their importance, multinational enterprises are marked, in the different development stages, by substantial qualitative

differences which are attributable to the different state of development of communications and transport as well as management techniques and intra-company control systems[16]. It is only due to progress made in these fields since the end of the second stage that the conditions were created for a far-reaching integration of the activities of geographically widespread and, in absolute terms, large component units into an overall entrepreneurial strategy and hence for the emergence of competition policy problems characteristic of this type of enterprise.

III. Extent of the phenomenon

1. Macroeconomic Level

13. The importance of multinational enterprises within the world economy and the extent of their actual or potential impact on overall economic development is evident from a comparison of the total value added of these enterprises with world gross national product as well as from a comparison of the total value of international production measured by the value of sales of the multinational's foreign affiliates with the total value of exports of all market economies. In 1971 the value added of all multinationals was estimated at $500 billion which corresponds to a share in world gross national product (excluding centrally planned economies) of approximately one-fifth[17]. Also in 1971 international production, defined as production subject to foreign control or decision and measured by the sales of foreign affiliates of multinational corporations, exceeded trade as the main vehicle of international economic exchange. It is estimated that international production reached approximately $330 billion in 1971. This was larger than total exports of all market economies[18]. In the light of more recent figures, the importance of multinationals is likely to have even increased since the estimated growth rate of international production in the past decade considerably exceeded[19] that of world gross national product and that of exports.

2. Microeconomic Level

14. Although the quantitative information on multinationals is still very incomplete some characteristic features of multinationals may be identified from it which are significant for any assessment in terms of competition policy. The first point to be made is the large absolute size of such enterprises which indicates their competitive strength. Here the general statement can be made that the majority of enterprises belonging to the top size class of any rank order based on criteria such as turnover or capital employed are multinationals. The 650 largest industrial enterprises of the market economies, of which as many as 146 operate branches in at least 7 countries, are nearly all multinationals within the definition adopted here[20].

15. The positive relationship between firm size and activity abroad is also reflected in the heavy concentration of direct investment by a few enterprises. According to studies made by the United States Department of Commerce in the 1950s, about 6 per cent of all enterprises investing abroad accounted for close to 80 per cent of investment abroad by United States enterprises, and this figure of 6 per cent included the largest enterprises in the sectors which carried out the bulk of the investment abroad[21]. More recent studies show a similar picture. According to them, 187 United States enterprises accounted for 80 per cent of all direct foreign investment in manufacturing industry (excluding production facilities in Canada), and these 187 enterprises belonged to the group of the 500 largest United States industrial corporations[22].

16.   Other countries which are also among the major exporters of investment capital show an even higher concentration of direct investment by a small number of enterprises.   In Germany, for example, 2 per cent of the firms investing abroad accounted for 70 per cent of direct investment[23] on average over the past few years, and the nine largest foreign investors alone controlled 37 per cent of the total[24].   In the United Kingdom, 165 firms accounted for 80 per cent of total direct investment abroad[25].

17.   The finding that firms operating abroad are as a rule larger than average does not answer the question as to what extent foreign affiliates rely on the resources of the enterprise as a whole in competing.   This question may be left open, however, since the foreign affiliates themselves usually hold important positions from the competition point of view.   This is most obvious in Canada where 75 of the 100 largest firms are under foreign control[26].   In Germany nearly one-half of direct foreign investment is made in firms with a nominal capital of DM.100 million and over (1970: 59 firms[28]).   In Italy, foreign corporations are on average four times as large as domestic companies[28].   In Belgium, foreign firms account for 28.6 per cent of the firms employing 1,000 persons or more, while representing only 1.6 per cent of all firms[29].   37 per cent of the foreign firms in Belgium have no competitors there, and 19 per cent are faced only with competition from other foreign firms operating in Belgium[30].   In the United Kingdom, of the 500 largest firms of that country, 45 are subsidiaries of United States corporations[31].   Another 13 of these 500 largest firms are subsidiaries of the Fortune "200 Largest Industrials Outside the U.S."[32].   In the United States direct foreign inward investment is equally concentrated among a few firms[33].   Studies in France showed a slight tendency towards concentration of foreign-owned enterprises among the larger industries in France[34].   In the developping countries, finally, subsidiaries of multinationals often have even more important strategic positions from the competition point of view[35].

18.   Furthermore, markets on which multinationals typically operate show specific structural characteristics[36].   A distinction has to be made between so-called horizontal or import substituting direct investments by multinationals serving the production or the sale in the host country of identical or similar products as are made by the parent company, and so-called vertical direct investments which are characterised by the fact that the products made by means of these investments are mainly destined for sale or processing in other countries.

19.   The multinational enterprises which make horizontal direct investments typically belong to technologically advanced and research-based industries or those industries which offer branded consumer goods for which there is a high income elasticity of demand in the host countries.   Moreover, the markets in the parent companies' home countries and the markets of the host countries are generally characterised by above-average degrees of concentration as well as high capital intensities and above-average growth rates ; in other words, the market structure of heterogeneous oligopoly and high entry barriers is often characteristic of the home and foreign markets of multinationals making horizontal direct investments.   The industries which typically show these characteristics and in which the degree of internationalisation of production is particulary marked include above all the automobile, electric and chemical industries, rubber and asbestos processing, mechanical engineering and food, drink and tobacco.

20.   To the extent that vertical direct investment is made in manufacturing industries, this is explained primarily by comparative cost differences.   In these cases investments are preferably made in developing countries having already reached an advanced stage of development, where sufficiently skilled labour is available on a large scale and where wage costs are relatively low.   The products made by the foreign branches in these countries are generally standardized and labour-intensive industrial products (among

others, electronic and textile products) which make comparatively small demands on the training level of the workers and are largely intended for processing or for sale in other countries.

21. More significiant for competition policy than cost-induced production shifting is the class of vertical direct investment by multinationals which links the extraction of a natural ressource in one country to its processing or fabrication in another country. Production conditions at the processing level and often at the extractive level are characterised by a high capital-intensity, a high capital need in absolute terms, and a long capital engagement period. As with import-substituting industries, the industries making vertical direct investments (among others, mineral oil processing and aluminium production) are characterised by above-average degrees of concentration which in these cases can be explained above all by the production conditions prevailing in these sectors.

IV. Explanations for the formation of multinationals

22. The recently developed microeconomic explanations for private direct foreign investment stem from the failure of traditional theory to account for modern developments. For example numerous studies reveal[37] that direct investments made by multinationals show features inconsistent with the flows which would be predicted by international differences in interest rates. In particular, the following features are involved:

- Enterprises investing abroad often borrow capital there when it is available.
- Direct investment is concentrated in specific industries though in many different countries. If interest differentials between markets determined capital movements, one would expect that capital investment would be concentrated in specific countries and that it would be spread over many different industries.
- Direct investments between two countries often flow in opposite directions within the same industry.
- The control motive, i.e. the fact that direct as well as portfolio investments are made cannot be explained by the interest rate theory.

23. The failure of macroeconomically oriented explanations led to the development of approaches which try to explain the direction and structure of direct investments made by multinational enterprises by means of the theory of enterprise and the theory of industrial organisation. Both start from the finding that imperfections in the markets for goods and factors triggered off the internationalisation of production[38]. The question as to the extent to which direct investments contribute to eliminating or aggravating these market imperfections is answered in various ways.

24. It is generally accepted that the basic reason for the formation and growth of multinational enterprises, as in the case of most business enterprises, is the desire for profits or growth for the purpose of enterprise income maximisation, either in the short or long term. Such strategies as increasing turnover or diversification of enterprise activities are usually aimed at these overall long-term ends.

25. The findings of an empirical survey[39] of motives for direct investment showed that these motives fell into the following groups:

- developing, maintaining and strengthening market positions ;
- considerations of cost and location ;
- safeguarding raw material supplies ;
- state assistance measures (subsidisation or investment incentives).

Direct investments based on the first group of motives are by far the most important ; considerations of cost and location make up an increasing share of overall direct investments, whereas direct investments for reasons of safeguarding raw material supplies show a relative downward trend. State assistance measures may influence investment decisions but constitute the determining factor only in rare cases. Other factors which may affect the location of foreign investment are variations in taxation and the desire to avoid trade barriers.

V. Economic analysis – competitive consequences in general

26. The impact of multinationals on competition has been viewed very differently. On the one hand it has been suggested that their activity has generally had a stimulating effect on competition[40], whereas other authors contend that there have been anticompetitive effects such as an increase in concentration in the markets where they operate[41]. However, firm conclusions do not seem possible for three reasons: the lack of systematic and complete data ; the widely varying size, nature and behaviour of multinational enterprises, broadly defined ; and the lack of analysis of the extent to which the specific multinational character of these enterprises is the reason for their effects on competition. In the light of this analysis, it is only possible to conclude that multinationals may affect the competitive process as regards its different elements – i.e. market structure, conduct and performance – positively as well as negatively.

27. In terms of competition policy one of the positive aspects of the internationalisation of production is that multinationals, as compared with national enterprises, may be more capable of entering concentrated national markets which are characterised by high entry barriers. Multinational enterprises may overcome market entry barriers and increase the number of suppliers even where barriers to entry are due to economies of scale as well as to product differentiation and absolute cost advantages. Thus, multinationals are in a more advantageous position as against national enterprises where economies of scale are significant only at one stage of production in that they can concentrate the production process in question at one single location and from there supply subsidiaries in different markets thereby overcoming the cost barriers which prevent entry by national enterprises[42].

28. Product differentiation is an obstacle to entry in that potential suppliers must either engage in advertising, which would require large and long-term capital expenditure, or lower their selling prices below those of established suppliers, which would then not be sufficient to cover average costs. Multinationals are in a better position to overcome market entry barriers caused by product differentiation since the exploitation of advantages arising from specific know-how in this field is one of the main reasons for the internationalisation of production[43].

29. According to Bain, absolute cost advantages which enable established enterprises to fix their prices more or less above average costs without market entry becoming profitable for newcomers are mainly due to the following:
   - "control of superior production techniques by established firms, maintained either by patents or by secrecy ;
   - exclusive ownership by established firms of superior deposits of resources required in production ;
   - inability of entrant firms to acquire necessary factors of production (management services, labour force, materials) on terms as favourable as those enjoyed by established firms ;

– less favoured access of entrant firms to liquid funds for investment reflected in higher effective interest costs or in simple unavailability of funds in the required amounts."[44].

30. A number of features of multinational enterprises facilitates their overcoming this type of barrier to entry: their generally high standard of technological and organisational know-how, their larger and better resources, their easier access to the capital markets of different countries, their absolute size, their possibility of subsidising market entry from profits obtained in other markets, etc. The multinationals' market entry through new establishments may therefore lead to increased competition and hence to an improved market performance resulting from an improved market structure brought about by a reduction in the degree of concentration.

31. Even in cases where the degree of concentration remains unchanged or increases as a result of market entry by a multinational enterprise the overall effect may also be to improve competition. This is evident where market entry is effected by taking over a domestic enterprise which otherwise would have disappeared from the market, for example, because of inefficient management. The positive result in terms of competition policy consists in its structure-preserving effect. However, it can also be considered an improvement in the sense of structural streamlining when the market entry of a multinational enterprise leads to the elimination of marginally profitable enterprises even though this increases concentration. In this case, however, for an overall positive assessment it is necessary that a sufficiently large number of competitive suppliers or buyers remain in the market concerned to ensure that productivity gains are spread at least partly throughout the economy. The examples illustrate that the assessment of direct investment in the light of simple criteria such as "investment for new enterprises, but not for take-overs" may have unsatisfactory results in terms of competition policy, which can be avoided only by means of a case-by-case assessment[45].

32. Apart from the impact of multinational enterprises on market structure, their influence on market conduct is particularly important when taking into account that even in the case of a concentration-reducing market entry the oligopolistic market structure as a rule continues to exist although it may be somewhat loosened. The positive effects of the structural improvement would only be limited if the multinational enterprises, instead of engaging in active competition, adjusted to the "stable pattern of oligopolistic interdependence or mutual accommodation that will normally evolve among a market's long-term tenants"[46].

33. Attempts to reach firm conclusions about multinationals' behaviour on oligopolistic markets by analysing their corporate structure and its influence on their motivation, information resources and range of opportunities have so far been unsatisfactory[47]. Considering the fact, however, that multinationals mainly operate on fast growing markets or, by entering a market and bringing in new products and manufacturing processes, stimulate growth, they are rather to be expected to engage in active competition, including competition in prices. Expanding markets are characterised by a lesser degree of interdependence on the part of oligopolists than markets in the phase of stagnation or recession[48]. During the growth phase, high price elasticity of overall demand allows the individual firm even to use the means of price policy in order to improve its proceeds without creating the risk of cut-throat competition. Examples of active price policies by multinationals which were not directed at eliminating competitors will be given below[49]. On the whole, however, the use of other forms of competition such as advertising and promotion, product design, product and process innovation, organisation of distribution service, etc. seems to prevail over active pricing policies[50].

34.   The positive influence multinationals have on market structure and market conduct may, on balance, result in an improvement in market performance, even though the impact on the various components of the latter, i.e. technical and allocative efficiency, product design, quality and technological progress in the fields of organisation as well as product and process innovation, may differ. Advantages are likely to occur in particular in the field of technological progress[51] while there exists at the same time the danger of welfare losses as a result of excessive product differentiation.

35.   The positive effects multinationals may have on technical efficiency have already been pointed out in connection with the discussion of barriers to entry due to economies of scale. As regards the effects on allocative efficiency it has to be noted that above-average profit rates and/or prices which considerably exceed average costs and which may be found on markets where multinationals operate do not necessarily reflect poor performance. On the one hand such markets usually have high entry barriers and, in the absence of multinationals, would show either even higher profit rates or a larger extent of profit-concealing "organisational slack"[52]. On the other hand, high profit rates could, at least in part, "represent a return on past investments in creating capital in the form of knowledge which does not appear on the firm's books as an addition to material capital"[53].

36.   However, because of the economic power wielded by multinationals and the special structure of the markets on which they operate there is a danger of negative influences on the process of competition. With regard to market structures, a distinction can be drawn between directly and indirectly harmful effects. The factors which directly affect the market structure by increasing the degree of concentration include takeovers of competitors in already concentrated markets for the purpose of restricting competition as well as cases of predatory competition. Compared with national enterprises, multinational enterprises may have more opportunities to engage in predatory practices for various reasons. Thus, multinationals not only enjoy economies of scale and the possibility of international cross-subsidisation – which is also true of large diversified national groups – but also have a number of competitive advantages resulting from their transnational structure which are not based on efficiency. These advantages include in particular their special position on the factor markets. Due to the fact that they are relatively free to determine intra-group transfer prices and internal terms of payment ("leads and lags") very large multinationals may be able to counteract restrictive national monetary and credit policies. A further increase in cash flow can be realised by taking advantage of differences in national taxation systems, also by way of transfer prices. The multinationals' special position in the national labour market results from their being able to exert demand pressure because of their greater flexibility in respect of international transfers of production[54].

37.   The second group of (indirectly) harmful effects on market structures is not reflected in an increase in concentration, which may even decrease at least at the time of the multinationals' market entry. Thus Kindleberger mentions a possible case where "in a concentrated industry with foreign competitors in the American market an investment by a leading firm in the home market of its foreign rivals in the United States market conveys an implicit instruction not to rock the boat"[55]. Such defensive investments serve to increase the awareness of the oligopolists' interdependence on both the home and the host markets of directly investing multinationals and may therefore replace formal cartel agreements[56]. It has to be noted that the level of concentration may even be lowered by such measures.

38.   As regards the large multinationals' long-term structural effects it should be pointed out that the process of selection arising from normal market forces may be impaired because of their centralised decision making. If internal management decisions

replace those of competitive markets there is a danger that relative efficiency may not be reflected in market prices. Involuntary cross-subsidisation practised in very large multinational enterprises might eliminate efficient national suppliers from the market. This argument applies also to large diversified national enterprises, but in the case of multinationals it may be more significant because cross-subsidisation may be obscured by the different timing of cyclical movements in separate national markets.

39.   Also belonging to the group of possible indirect negative effects on the market structure are the cases of "export" of an oligopolistic market structure to the host country. Here, too, a distinction can be made between direct and indirect effects. As to the former, it is conceivable that enterprises whose national markets are highly concentrated might simultaneously make large direct investments in less developed countries with growing markets[57]. This form of oligopolistic parallel conduct could entail an overcrowding of the market concerned and efficiency losses. This could prevent the development of a less concentrated industry with fewer multinationals. This parallel conduct might be explained by the endeavour to maintain an oligopolistic equilibrium on the home market of the directly investing enterprise which would be jeopardised if an unforeseeable successful advance was made but which would not be affected if there was a general failure of parallel foreign investment.

40.   The indirect export of oligopolistic market structures refers to the situation where the multinationals' entry into less concentrated markets may trigger off a defensive concentration process among the enterprises of the host country. The merger wave observed in the mid-sixties in Western Europe is a least party explainable by the increasing penetration of United States enterprises which European enterprises considered to be a challenge[58] which could only be answered by increased external growth.

41.   Finally, the entry of multinationals may have negative effects on elements of market structure other than the horizontal degree of concentration. In particular, barriers to market entry may be further raised by international vertical concentration processes as well as by extensive advertising and product differentiation.

42.   As mentioned in connection with the description of the positive effects, the multinationals' impact on market conduct and performance depends to a large extent on the development phase of the market concerned. In an oligopolistic market where overall demand is stagnating or growing only moderately and the product is technologically mature, the use of entrepreneurial action parameters shifts competition to areas inferior in terms of welfare economics, such as excessive advertising, inflationary product differentiation, excessive research expenditure with diminishing marginal returns, etc. Even in cases of significant cost-reducing innovations the price parameter is not used because of high oligopolistic interdependence.

43.   In conclusion, it can be stated that, from the point of view of competition, there is no presumption for or against multinationals. While in some circumstances the entry and behaviour of multinational enterprises in a new market has improved market structure and performance because of greater competition, in other cases the restrictive practices of particular multinational enterprises combined with their large size and market power have resulted in a serious reduction in economic welfare. As noted before it is not possible to make a balance of competitive effects. An attempt will however be made to describe to some extent the possible positive effects, and in greater detail, the various forms of restraints of competition by multinationals which have especially adverse effects on the economy. The latter will be discussed in greater detail in order to indicate the direction for any measures that may need to be taken in the field of competition policy.

VI. Procompetitive effects of multinationals

44. Experience confirms the hypothesis that the entry of foreign firms into markets dominated by one or a few domestic enterprises may stimulate competition simply as a result of the capacity effect caused by new establishments. This may lead to price reductions or at least prevent or weaken the rate of further price increases. The appearance of United States firms in the United Kingdom, for example, has resulted in the breaking up of virtual or potential monopolies for watches, tyres, soaps and detergents, radiators and boilers, clocks, office appliances, refrigeration machinery and excavating equipment[59]. Although in these cases the market entry of foreign firms only caused monopolistic positions to be replaced by oligopolies, the effect in several instances was to hold prices down during inflation or cut them further during price declines. The entry of Firestone and Goodyear into the French tyre market in 1962 forced Michelin, Dunlop and Kléber-Colombes to reduce their prices[60].

45. In Australia, foreign investors turned some local tobacco and detergents industries from monopoly into an oligopoly. The oligopolistic profits on these markets were diminished by the appearance of additional competitors and prices were kept down[61].

46. Caves, who made a statistical inquiry into the effects of the activities of foreign firms in Canadian manufacturing industries, arrived at an overall positive judgment, though with certain reservations[62]. According to his inquiry, the level of profits as a measure of allocative efficiency and thereby of the intensity of competition showed a weak tendency to vary inversely with the share of industry output held by foreign owned firms. On the other hand, there was no such correlation in unconcentrated industries or in industries where subsidiaries of multinational enterprises accounted for a small proportion of total output. As regards this result it has to be taken into account, however, that it was not possible to determine to what extent the inverse relationship between foreign share and profit rate was attributable to possibly inefficient plant sizes.

47. Furthermore, where foreign affiliates assume production of goods which so far had not been made in the host country, this may contribute indirectly to an improvement in the competitive situation on unrelated domestic markets. Such cases are shown by Gervaise[63] to have occurred in France. According to him, import substitution by the production of foreign affiliates led to an improvement in the balance of payments which then allowed trade policy to be liberalised ; trade liberalisation in turn increased import competition and reduced prices in the chemical, pharmaceutical, machinery and electronic sectors, among others.

VII. Anticompetitive effects of multinational enterprises

1. General Remarks

48. Although restrictive business practices attributed to multinational enterprises may not differ in form from those operated by purely national firms, their international character means that their impact on trade and competition is more significant. The reasons for this difference are to be found , as explained above, in their, on average, superior size, superior economic power, easier access to international financial markets and raw materials as well as in their superior technological and management standards. They also play a greater role in the process of concentration and in concentrated markets.

49.   The four main categories of restrictions identified in the remainder of this chapter are neither specific to multinational enterprises in the sense that they could and would not also be operated by purely national firms nor are they comprehensive in the sense that multinational enterprises could and would not also engage in other restrictive practices.   These categories have been chosen because they generally represent special areas of concern and because there seems to be sufficient evidence to demonstrate why they are particularly questionable when operated by multinationals.   Normally, different types of restrictions are applied together.   Therefore most of the following cases could be brought under two or more of these categories.   The attempt has however been made to classify cases according to the main restriction operated even though a certain degree of arbitrariness was unavoidable.   Within the different categories, except for mergers, a distinction between individual and collective practices has been used.   A restrictive practice is "individual" in this sense when it is operated by a single multinational enterprise, and "collective" when at least two multinational enterprises participate in it.

2.   International Allocation of Production and Markets

(a) Individual Market and Production Allocation

50.   Multinational enterprises, pursuing long-run global strategies of profit and growth maximisation as well as risk minimisation may individually restrict the range of products to be produced or the markets to be served by their component units in particular countries.   The means used include decisions respecting prices, investments and international commodity trade and other forms of action.   Patent and trademark licensing restrictions are often employed.   Such restrictions can have deleterious effects on the economy of the country where the unit is located.   Its industry may be prevented from producing goods for home consumption or export, which it is capable of producing competitively.   Where production for home consumption is involved, the country may have to import products which could be made domestically at lower cost.   It may furthermore be prevented from importing products from the lowest cost sources, with consequent adverse effects upon domestic price levels and productive efficiency.   On the other hand, since multinational enterprises may wish to create subsidiaries solely to exploit foreign markets and may be unwilling to create intra-enterprise competition within their existing markets a ban on the control of subsidiaries might deter their creation and thus decrease direct foreign investment.

51.   As for export restrictions imposed by parent companies on foreign subsidiaries, up to now only *Canada* has dealt with them as, inter alia, an issue of competition policy.   A study of foreign direct investment in Canada[64] analysed the export policy of 964 subsidiaries of foreign enterprises.   This study showed that 459 of the 798 subsidiaries controlled by United States interests were subject to some form or other of restriction on their exports.   In these cases, the most common restriction was exclusion from the United States market.   Of the remaining 166 subsidiaries controlled from abroad by other than United States firms, 72 were also under some form of export limitation.   In this connection the survey concedes that "in some cases these restrictions are merely an institutionalisation of the relative costs of production in Canada and elsewhere".   At the same time, however, it emphasizes that "in other cases they are real barriers to the achievement of increased production and economies of scale".   In this context mention should be made of a private study[65] concerning *United Kingdom* manufacturing subsidiaries in *Australia*, which found that almost half of the enterprises examined were subject to some form of export restriction.

52.   A *Canadian* report on farm tractors[66] issued by the Royal Commission on Farm Machinery illustrates the effectiveness of international market allocation schemes as

well as their economic significance. The Report found that, in 1966, three multinational enterprises, Massey-Ferguson, International Harvester and Ford, manufactured about half the production of farm tractors in the non-Communist world. North America accounted for about one-third of world production of tractors, most of the balance being produced in Western Europe where Britain took first place with about 26 per cent of total production. It would be expected that the absence of customs tariffs on farm tractors in Canada and in the United States would keep price differences between Canada and Europe within moderate limits, especially at the factory level. In fact, while free trade had eliminated the price differences that formerly existed between Canada and the United States, the Commission found substantial differences between Canada and the major Western European producing countries including the United Kingdom. Moreover, large differences existed at the level of sales to the Canadian subsidiaries of the manufacturers and were not related to differences in costs of domestic distribution.

53.   The pound sterling was devalued in November 1967 by about 14.3 per cent and the Royal Commission noted that virtually none of the effects of devaluation had been passed on in the form of lower prices in Canada. If the net factory price in England to the Canadian wholesale organisation had remained unchanged in pounds sterling the price to the Canadian subsidiaries would have declined by 14.3 per cent. In fact, the sterling prices to Canadian subsidiaries were apparently advanced by the full amount of the devaluation. The Royal Commission found that even before the British devaluation, prices of tractors to Canadian dealers were much higher than those paid by dealers in Great Britain and in a number of other countries in Western Europe. After devaluation the spread of tractors prices up to 75 hp increased and dealers in Britain paid between 30 and 45 per cent less than Canadian dealers for them.

54.   Some Canadian farmers attempted to buy tractors directly from British dealers but this trade was strongly resisted by the manufacturers. The Royal Commission found that all major tractor manufacturers had clauses in their dealers' contracts to prevent the latter from exporting new tractors directly or selling them to someone else who would export them. The Commission concluded that "the multinational corporations which dominate the farm machinery business closely control the movement of tractors and other farm machines from one country to another and set – on a fairly arbitrary basis – the prices at which these machines are supplied to their Canadian subsidiary". The report also recommended that efforts be made to find new sources of supplies other than Western Europe, but recognised that new suppliers might have serious difficulties in establishing dealer networks and dependable supplies of spare parts.

55.   The *Canadian* case of still picture projectors, which was one of the subjects of an inquiry by the Tariff Board into photographic equipment, is another instance of market allocation. Sales of Canadian produced still picture projectors were limited by foreign parent companies to the Canadian market except under special circumstances. The spokesman for a producer, Bell and Howell (Canada) Ltd., stated at a public hearing, that it was the practice of its parent firm to grant exclusive market territories to the subsidiary plants[67].

56.   A number of cases decided by the Commission of the *European Communities* illustrate how market-sharing strategies can be realised by compensatory payments[68]. Production restrictions, obligations to purchase specific raw materials and semimanufactures as well as conditions regarding delivery also serve to safeguard market and production allocations. There are cases, for example, where cheap raw materials are made available to the affiliated companies only, whereas other enterprises are required to purchase more refined and thus more expensive materials. It does not seem to be rare, however, as is illustrated for instance in the British and German Hoffman-La Roche cases[69], that subsidiaries which often play a dominant part on national markets,

have to buy the raw materials at a higher than competitive price. In *France*, there are also indications that a French subsidiary was obliged by its parent company located in the United States to purchase essential raw materials from a British affiliate of the same group at a higher price than the parent company itself charged other French buyers ; investigations however, are still continuing.

(b) Collective Market and Production Allocation

57. Multinational firms sometimes consolidate their economic power and draw advantages from it not only individually but also by means of agreements or concerted actions with other enterprises, particularly in oligopolies where most multinationals are to be found. Such agreements are facilitated by the possibility in many countries of legalising certain types of cartels: for example, rebate, rationalisation, import and specialisation cartels in which the subsidiaries of multinational firms may participate[70] and which may, and in fact sometimes do, serve as the nucleus for an international system of restrictive agreements. This may in particular be the case for national and international export cartels[71].

58. Legal and illegal allocation of markets or production within cartel agreements is frequently effected – as is for example shown by a Canadian investigation[72]– by the division or allocation of "hunting grounds" to individual firms and the designation of so-called "open markets" on which there may exist some degree of competition. A widespread form of market sharing is the use of home protection clauses[73] or so-called preferential areas as well as the recognition of established supply relationships. Such allocative practices, which may be employed by subsidiaries after a directive from the parent company, require some kind of co-ordination and control as do the corresponding individual restrictive practices.

59. Although there is insufficient evidence to assess precisely the role of multinational firms in export cartels on an industry by industry basis or to quantify exactly their economic significance, it can be concluded from an internal study of the Federal Cartel Office that multinationals participate in approximately 70 per cent of all *German* export cartels. An analysis of 41 international export cartels in the *United Kingdom* (32 per cent of total export cartels) indicated that 20 out of 29 cartels with multinational participation had both British and foreign multinational members. A peculiar problem of the presence of multinational enterprises in permitted export cartels is that such enterprises may belong to such cartels in more than one country and may be able to influence or limit competition among such export groups.

60. *United Kingdom* experience, which roughly corresponds to that of Germany, indicates – as shown in the following table – that export cartels are widely used in highly concentrated industries[74] in which multinationals are most frequently to be found.

U.K. Active Export Cartels and Industrial Concentration[75]

5-Firm Concentration Ratio %	Number of Export Cartels
1 – 33	14
34 – 66	38
67 – 100	78
	130

These data suggest that there is a high degree of multinational co-operation particularly that consisting of the participation of multinational enterprises in export cartels.

61. The table on the following page shows the percentage frequency of restrictions found in *78 German*[76] *export cartels* (39 national and 39 international) in which multinational enterprises were involved (as of 31st December, 1974).

62. Most export cartel agreements provide for some kind of control to ensure that the agreements are observed and for some type of sanction in cases of violation. In a large number of cases, international cartel organisations in the form of trust offices, management or pricing committees, for example, not only function as reporting centres but also provide procedures for giving prior consent to tenders and for concluding contracts.

63. Just as national cartels or agreements may lead to an international system of restraints of competition, so may international co-operation give rise to national cartelisation. The Water-Tube Boilermaker's Association Case[77] and the Scan Organisations Case[78] are typical examples of this interdependence of domestic and international cartels. Both agreements provided for home market protection as well as co-operation in regard to exports. To be mentionned in this context is also the obligation accepted by a German multinational firm in an international export cartel to induce other German companies engaged in domestic and foreign trade not to undercut the cartel's export prices[79].

Percentage Frequency of Restrictions Found in German Export Cartels
(as of 31st December, 1974)

	Price fixing	Fixing of rebates	Fixing of conditions	Fixing of quotas	Exclusive or preferential dealing	Ad hoc and/or collusive tendering	Open price systems	Pooling of profits	Joint ventures
International Export Cartels	76	18	67	59	13	8	28	21	13
National Export Cartels	15	5	76	31	–	21	28	8	15

3. *International Pricing Abuses and Other Forms of Abuses of Economic Power*

a) *Individual Abuses*

64. A generally decisive factor for the enforcement of abusive pricing strategies is the economic power of the enterprise concerned within the market in question. If the latter is of an oligopolistic nature competition is frequently lessened even without formal agreements between the oligopolists simply by virtue of their oligopolistic interdependence. The danger of higher prices being charged than would be obtained if competition existed is obvious. Even if competition authorities suspect such practies it is often difficult to find out whether they exist or not.

65. Another practice which has raised concern is the practice of international predatory pricing, which involves the supply of goods and services to a particular country at prices below cost for a certain period in order to drive competitors out of business. Anti-dumping laws – which only exist in some countries – may fail to prevent such practices when there exists neither a comparable market in the goods allegedly dumped nor effective enforcement by national authorities.

66. Similar effects can be achieved when multinationals control the sources or the marketing of raw materials and charge higher prices to competing producers or dealers in the finished products. A number of *Irish importers* of bananas for example have

recently complained that competition on the market is being distorted through the activities of a multinational ; they allege that bananas are being made available at an uneconomic price with a view to the eventual achievement of a monopoly on the Irish banana market.

67.   International price differentiation, i.e. the creation and/or exploitation of different price levels in different countries by multinational enterprises is found in many instances. Particularly if the differences are considerable and not based on differences in costs or competitive conditions, they may indicate the existence of abusive high prices in one or more countries.

68.   A 1963 report on the drug manufacturing industry[80] in *Canada*, which industry consists largely of subsidiaries of foreign multinationals, found that consumer prices of 58 drugs were 3 to 20 times higher than the corresponding retail prices in Britain. A possible explanation for this that there were lower manufacturing costs in particular countries did not hold in this case. The Minister of Consumer and Corporate Affairs stated in the House of Commons on 13th February, 1968: "In many cases these companies have been able to use patents to prevent the entry by others into production of individual drugs. They have substituted for price competition the development of minor differences in the product and vigorous sales promotion of these small differences. We are now in a position to explain why the level of Canadian drug prices is amongst the highest in the world. Because of the heavily protected position enjoyed by the producers, drug pricing is based chiefly on demand. The policy of charging what the traffic will bear can be followed. This means that drug prices will be the highest in those countries where the per capita income is the highest. The alternative explanation that drugs are sold at lower prices in foreign countries because production costs are lower does not stand up to factual examination. It is quite common to see a drug that is manufactured in the United States and exported to a European country selling much more cheaply in that country than in the United States[81]. Some forms of international price discrimination may injure competition by weakening competitors of the discriminating firm or by distorting competition among competing firms which resell the product subject to the discrimination. Also some forms of international price discrimination may indicate that direct injury to consumers is occurring.

69.   Another example of price discrimination affecting inter-State commerce within the *European Communities* can be found in the EEC Commission's decision of the W.E.A. Fillipacchi Music S.A. case[82]. This company, 51 per cent of which is controlled by the United States firm, Warner Brothers Inc., and 39 per cent by the Banque Rothschild, was fined for having prevented its French record distributors from exporting to Germany in order to maintain a substantial artificial price difference between the two countries. The company sold in France the most usual type of record for about 14 francs, whereas the same records were sold in Germany by its German subsidiary for DM. 14 [Smithsonian central rates FF.5.12 = DM. 3.22]. When French dealers started to export records to Germany, WEA Fillipacchi S.A. attempted to force its French customers to guarantee that no records would be exported to Germany by third parties so as to reserve the market for its German subsidiary.

70.   The substantially higher prices of tractors found in *Canada*[83] and *Sweden*[84] as compared with other western industrial nations are also clearly a result of corporate policies taking advantage of differing price levels in different countries. The establishment of such systems of private non-tariff barriers to trade by multinational enterprises may thus frustrate governmental trade liberalisation policies and furthermore facilitate the exploitation of consumers as these cases illustrate.

71.   Authorities which have to prevent pricing abuses are confronted with a particular problem in the case of transfer prices. It is evident that transfer prices cannot be ac-

cepted as costs for the subsidiaries without justification. Nevertheless, the burden of proof on the side of national cartel authorities has been particularly heavy in these cases. Recent examples are to be found in the oil and pharmaceutical sectors.

72. During both the Suez crisis of 1967 and the oil crisis of 1973-74, the German Federal Cartel Office was unable to determine whether the price increases demanded and enforced by multinational oil companies were actually caused by cost increases or by an abuse of their market dominating position. While the Office knew the prices which were paid by individual subsidiaries for freight and for crude oil from different origins these transfer prices were fixed by the trading companies of the international oil groups without necessarily reflecting the actual cost conditions. As a result of the disparity in profits between the German subsidiaries and their parent companies, the suspicion was aroused that the trading companies charged their affiliates in the Federal Republic of Germany considerably higher prices for their supplies that were justifiable in the light of the increased costs for purchasers of oil. In 1973 the profits of the leading oil companies as presented by their subsidiaries in Germany were higher than their subsidiaries'turnover. Whereas the latter recorded a profit in 1973 it had occurred for the most part in the first three quarters. The losses shown by most of them for the fourth quarter compared with increases in the profits of the parent companies of between 50 and 70 per cent compared with the fourth quarter of 1972. In 1974 these discrepancies even increased. While a British Company quadrupled its profits in the first half of 1974 as against the same period the year before, the profit of its German subsidiary had been negative in every single month from January to June. It has not been possible to clear up these disparities since basic data on the multinational groups could not be obtained.

73. According to findings of the *French* authorities, the French subsidiaries of multinational oil companies sought to raise the price level through concerted action and to maintain it by fixing market shares, allocating orders and taking retaliatory measures against independent wholesalers disturbing the functioning of this cartel.

74. In addition to the above-mentioned increase in the price level of mineral oil products during the energy crisis between October 1973 and March 1974, another cause for concern in Germany was the simultaneous appearance of split prices for some of these products, which placed the independent wholesalers and filling stations at a disadvantage. Whereas the German subsidiaries of the multinational oil companies were able to charge relatively lower prices, the independent wholesalers were for the most part forced to buy at the comparatively high Rotterdam import prices. This high price level which was passed on to the independent filling stations restricted the latter's competitiveness considerably so that many independent filling stations had to be closed or affiliated to one of the oil groups. As a result the market share of independent filling stations declined from 25 per cent to approximately 15 per cent over a period of nine months. Because of their origin outside the area of application of the Act, it was impossible for the Federal Cartel Office to determine to what extent the high import prices to independent wholesalers had been influenced by the foreign affiliates of the international mineral oil groups.

75. The conclusions contained in the report of the *Commission of the European Communities* on the behaviour of the oil companies in the Community during the period from October 1973 to March 1974[85] recalled firstly, in relation to the prices charged by the oil companies, that the transfer prices applied by the major oil companies did not fall within the rules of competition of the Treaty of Rome to the extent that the effects of such prices were purely internal to the enterprises. The report also indicated that the Commission did not find any agreements or concerted practices between the oil companies by comparing their respective transfer prices for crude and refined oil. In Ger-

many, in view of the highly diversified supply arrangements and the market economy which prevailed there, the Commission came to the conclusion that no oil company was able to abuse its dominant position during the period considered. Finally, the Commission said that it would continue to check whether the information system used by Platt's Oilgram did not result in prices being published which did not correspond to the whole of the actual quotations.

76.   A report by the *United Kingdom* Monopolies Commission[86] which had been asked to make an investigation after Roche Products had refused to participate in the United Kingdom Voluntary Price Regulation Scheme (VPRS) for National Health Service drugs, concluded that the transfer prices within the Hoffman-La Roche group of the active ingredients for two tranquilliser drugs, Librium and Valium, and also the overall level of profits on these drugs, were excessively high, and the Commission recommended a substantial reduction in the prices of these drugs.   The company challenged the validity of the conclusions of the Monopolies Commission report both in the United Kingdom Parliament and in the Courts.   However, negotiations were subsequently taken up out of court, which in due course led to a settlement between Roche and the British Government.   The central points of this settlement were that Roche agreed to adhere retroactively to the VPRS, accepting and being entitled to all consequences of this move.   (For example the VPRS operates on overall rather than individual product profitability).   In consequence the company agreed to repay £ 3.75 million to the United Kingdom Government covering the period 1970-1973 in respect of high profits in the period before the Price Order, less an adjustment for rising costs and lower profits during the period of the ordered price reduction.   The Government in return withdrew the Price Order and the company dropped its legal actions against the Government.   As a result of the settlement and in the light of additional information provided by Roche, price increases for Valium and Librium were permitted which took account of their current cost/profit position.

77.   A large part of the findings made by the United Kingdom Monopolies Commission was also true for the *German* drug market. The transfer prices which the parent company charged its German subsidiary amounted to 90 times the Italian competitive price of the active ingredient for Valium and to 47 times the Italian competitive price of the active ingredient for Librium.   The retail prices of the two drugs which exceeded those in the United Kingdom even prior to the officially ordered price cuts included a considerable amount of overheads which could not have been included if effective competition prevailed.   On the grounds that it had abused its dominating market position for these drugs – the market share together with two other firms was found by the Federal Cartel Office to amount to approximately 94 per cent and by the Berlin Court of Appeals to approximately 85 per cent of the retail pharmacists' business – the FCO ordered the enterprise to cut its selling prices by between 35 and 40 per cent.   The Berlin Court of Appeals confirmed the decision of the Federal Cartel Office on its merits, but it fixed a higher abuse limit with regard to the research activities of Hoffmann-La Roche.   Hoffmann-La Roche and the Federal Cartel office have appealed to the Federal Supreme Court against this decision. The price reduction has not yet come into force as requests for a preliminary injunction to this end have been refused twice by the Berlin Court of Appeals.

78.   In other Member countries – *France, Norway* and the *Netherlands* – proceedings have also been instituted against this firm for abusive pricing. Before the proceedings ended in the Netherlands the firm cut its prices there by 25 per cent. In Norway, the proceedings have also led to price cuts.

79.   In addition to these various forms of pricing abuses there are other types of individual restraints of competition resulting from the economic power enjoyed by mul-

tinational enterprises and affecting third parties. Numerous cases of refusals to sell by Norwegian-based subsidiaries of multinational firms may be mentioned in this context, for instance in the household appliances, vacuum cleaners and radio and TV sectors. The refusals were designed to have and had the effect of lessening competition and of keeping price levels high.

80. Discriminatory treatment has also been practised by multinational firms in various countries not only in regard to prices. Experience in several countries in connection with the oil crisis of 1973-1974 illustrates the economic significance of this type of restriction when operated by multinational enterprises. These discriminatory practices of multinational oil firms not only served to ensure high prices but also, as is shown by the experience in the *Netherlands*, to change existing market structures in their favour. In the Netherlands the international oil companies claimed during the crisis to be no longer in a position to supply a central buying association of 19 independent wholesalers due to existing contractual obligations. Some multinational enterprises indicated their readiness to continue supplies to certain wholesalers if the latter concluded longer-term agreements and gave up their independent status[87]. In a similar case in the *Federal Republic of Germany*, in which the German subsidiary of a multinational oil company justified its refusal to supply by referring to its obligation to supply its own network of filling stations, the Berlin Court of Appeals ruled also that unequal treatment was in principle illegal[88].

81. Another phenomenon reflecting the economic power of international firms is the use of tying agreements which are occasionally found in times of short supply and where there exist long-term supply relationships. Such agreements are restrictive not only in that they increase customers' dependence and unduly restrict the latter's economic freedom of choice but also insofar as tying agreements strengthen barriers to market entry by third parties and stabilize existing market structures[89].

b) Collective Abuses

82. Apart from individual practices, multinational enterprises may also create or take advantage of differing price levels in different countries by collective action, for example within the framework of international cartels. The economic significance of such concerted action is illustrated by a number of important international cartel cases such as the EC dyestuffs and quinine cartel cases. By "artifically reducing the possibilities of mutual penetration of the individual markets at the consumer level"[90] multinational enterprises may, as in the EC dyestuffs case, largely eliminate price as a major parameter of competition. This latter case illustrates at the same time the effectiveness of a concerted price increase if carried out by multinationals.

83. Common price increases[91], agreed raising of the lower prices of imported goods to a higher domestic price level[92] and the contractual obligation not to sell at lower prices than the major manufacturers on individual markets[93] are other types of collectively applied restrictive practices of multinational enterprises. Within the quinine cartel, for example, the participating firms enforced common price increases on foreign and home markets. The effectiveness of the price increases was strengthened by market sharing and quota agreements, restrictions on the production of individual firms, common purchasing of raw materials ("bark pool") and a ban on co-operation with non-members in the manufacture or sale of quinine products.

84. It should be noted that the reported involvement of multinational enterprises in illegal international cartel activities appears to be considerably less frequent than the occurrence of illegal cartels found locally. This may be due to the superior legal counselling available to large, sophisticated firms or to failures of detection or relative lack of enforcement.

25

4. Anti-competitive Mergers

85.   The immediate and obvious effect of an international merger[94] in terms of competition policy, which under the definition used here, is either effected by or engenders a multinational enterprise is that it increases overall world concentration although it does not necessarily affect national levels of market and overall concentration. So, for example, a merger between two independent companies located in different countries may not necessarily increase concentration in either of the individual markets but does increase concentration if both markets are taken together.   Hence if the foreign enterprise involved in the merger is a potential competitor on the market supplied by the domestic enterprise, a merger policy that is only based upon the criterion of the national market share would lead to unsatisfactory results for the safeguarding of a competitive situation.   On the other hand, if the foreign enterprise acquires a relatively small, minor or unsuccessful firm in the national market and employs its acquisition for the development of a strong position, this strategy may produce most of the benefits of independent entry or, at least, cause no harm.

86.   At the present time, it is difficult to assess the impact of multinational enterprises on the world-wide degree of concentration because sufficiently comprehensive information is still not available. This is due to the fact that most countries do not gather or publish data on mergers.   As shown by an analysis of notified mergers in those countries which have such a system, purely national mergers account for the major part of total merger activity.   The ratio of international/purely national mergers, however, differs considerably from one country to another.

87.   In *Canada*, for example, international mergers were on average 35 per cent of the total number of mergers over the period 1960 to 1974 and 29 per cent for the 3–year period 1972–1974, which were highest in an inter-country comparison. There is no discernible trend in the movement of relative shares.   For *Sweden*, the corresponding figures were 15 per cent in 1969, approximately 8 per cent in 1970, 15 per cent in 1971, and 8 per cent in 1972.   In the *Netherlands,* a marked trend in the number of national and international mergers can be noticed over the period 1966 to 1971. Thus, the ratio of mergers involving foreign firms was 17 per cent in 1966, 19 per cent in 1967, 22 per cent in 1968, 29 per cent in 1969, 22 per cent in 1970, 25 per cent in 1971 and 40 per cent in 1972[95].   In *Germany*, the share of international mergers in the total number of mergers notified to the Federal Cartel Office varied between 12 and 23 per cent in each year from 1966 to 1972.   The average share over the entire period was approximately 20 per cent.   In 1973 it rose to 31 per cent and to about 34 per cent in 1974. Reliable trend forecasts are, however, not yet possible in Germany.   In the *United Kingdom*, mergers involving the acquisition of a British company by a foreign-owned company amounted to an average of about 10 per cent of the total number of merger projects examined by the Monopolies Commission over the period 1965 to mid-1974.   Here, too, it does not seem possible to detect any trend[96].

88.   These figures, however, do not say much about the competitive impact of mergers involving multinational enterprises in that they do not indicate the relative importance of foreign mergers either in terms of the assets or market shares acquired or persons employed.   Due to the lack of relevant data in most countries, this question has been analysed but rarely up to now.   One of the studies to be mentioned in this context covers the development in Canada during the years 1945 to 1961[97]. Rosenbluth comes to the conclusion, among others, that multinational enterprises accounted for a disproportionately high amount of merger activity in selected industries compared with domestic firms (manufacturing petroleum and natural gas, mining and smelting,

railways, utilities, merchandising) and that a marked increase in the percentage of capital controlled by foreign interests was discernible in these industries.

89.   Taking account of the Canadian experience and the fact that multinational enterprises are on average larger in absolute terms than national enterprises, their merger activities in some countries have a substantially stronger impact on the competitive process than could be inferred from their share in the total number of merger cases. This conclusion is also supported by other observations. As already mentioned above, a number of studies have shown that multinational enterprises typically operate on markets that are concentrated both in the home and the host country and on markets that are characterised by high entry barriers[98]. Mergers occurring in such markets are particularly questionable from the competition policy point of view. The presumption that the merger activities of multinational enterprises are responsible for concentration processes undesirable in terms of competition policy to an extent far greater than can be gathered from their share in the total number of merger cases, is further supported by experience gained in Germany since the introduction of merger control in 1973. Multinational enterprises were there involved in four of the five cases in which the merger   was prohibited because it was likely to create or strengthen a market dominating position.

90.   An overall assessment of the impact of multinational enterprises on national concentration ratios requires a comparative analysis of the new establishements set up by these firms. The empirical evidence available for such an analysis is still rather scarce. In 1974 a study was published by the Harvard Business School on the 187 largest United States and the 226 largest non-United States multinational enterprises[99]. According to this study, United States firms had, as of 1st January, 1968, preferred to acquire shares in already existing companies in the nine EC countries in 814 out of 1451 cases (equalling 56.1 per cent) rather than to found new establishments. This form of market entry was chosen even more often by non-United States firms. As of 1st January, 1971, 1073 out of a total of 1694 in the EC (equalling 63.3 per cent) were acquisitions of existing firms.

91.   The external growth of multinational enterprises by means of acquisitions is also the most important method used in developing countries. In a paper prepared for the UNIDO based on a census of the 396 world's leading transnational corporations as of 1st January, 1968, 54.9 per cent of the manufacturing subsidiaries of 187 United States-based transnational corporations in developing countries became affiliated by acquisition[100]. The corresponding percentage for 209 transnational corporations also based elsewhere is 58.7 per cent. The UNIDO survey also points out that acquisitions were relatively more common after 1959 than before, and slightly more common in Asia and Africa than in Latin America.

92.   The following selection of international merger cases involving multinational enterprises illustrates their economic and competitive consequences. The cases have been subject to specific control proceedings by the competent national authorities because they had or were expected to have restrictive effects on competition in the countries concerned. In considering these cases it should be kept in mind that national merger control aims at supervising concentration movements within the respective national markets. For this reason, examples of mergers which only increase worldwide concentration and restrict international competition without also having perceptible restrictive effects on national markets cannot be reported in this context. Such cases may escape totally the attention of national cartel authorities and since there is no other source of adequate information available at the present time, it is not possible to draw definite conclusions as regards the importance of such mergers in absolute terms.

93.   A case illustrating the difficulty of judging the anti-competitive consequences of international mergers by multinational enterprises is the *Continental Can Company* case of the EC commission and the European Court of Justice. In 1969 the Continental Can Company had already acquired 85 per cent of the share capital of the largest German producer of light metal containers, Schmalbach-Lubeka Werke A.G. One year later it acquired through its Belgian subsidiary, Europemballage Corporation S.A., the Dutch company Thomassen en Drijver Verblifa N.V., the largest producer of light metal containers within the Benelux countries at that time. As regards this second acquisition, the Commission found in its decision of 1971[101], that it had the effect of eliminating in practice competition in a substantial part of the EC light metal container market, and, therefore, constituted an abuse of a dominant position in the sense of Article 86 of the EEC Treaty. Two years later, the European Court of Justice confirmed in principle the interpretation that the Commission had given to this Article but repealed the latter's decision on the grounds that it had not sufficiently defined the relevant market[102].

94.   One of the main effects which horizontal international mergers may have is to increase barriers to market entry.   The merger of *Johnson & Johnson and Hahn* prohibited by the German Federal Cartel Office had this detrimental effect, in the Office's opinion[103]. In this case, the United-States based multinational company, Johnson & Johnson, New Brunswick, making hospital supplies, hygienic, cosmetic and pharmaceutical products and distributing them almost all over the world, acquired, in the summer of 1973, a majority interest in the German enterprise, Dr. Carl Hahn GmbH of Düsseldorf. Prior to the merger, Hahn was a non-affiliated company producing mainly hygienic and cosmetic articles. With a market share of about 80 per cent it dominates the German tampon market. It was to be expected that the merger would have consolidated Hahn's dominating position on the German tampon market. The Federal Cartel Office found that, because of Hahn's access to the superior financial and research resources of Johnson & Johnson, and its greater experience in sales promotion techniques market entry barriers to other enterprises would have been correspondingly raised if the merger had been allowed. The decision of the Federal Cartel Office, however, was reversed by the Berlin Court of Appeals for procedural reasons. The Federal Cartel Office has lodged an appeal on points of law to the Federal Supreme Court against the Court's decision.

95.   The proposed *AEG – Telefunken/Zanussi*[104] merger would have been prohibited by the German Federal Cartel Office if it had not been abandoned by the firms themselves, because it would have led to an anticompetitive vertical concentration.
AEG – Telefunken, a company domiciled in the Federal Republic of Germany, planned to purchase a share of 25.01 per cent in the Italian firm Industrie A. Zanussi S.p.A. This holding was intended to secure and strengthen existing co-operation and AEG – Telefunken's financial management in Zanussi in the field of household appliances (washing machines etc.). Its holding in Zanussi and its position as a major customer would have allowed AEG – Telefunken to exercise substantial influence on Zanussi's business policy as far as exports of household appliances to the German market were concerned. On the other hand, AEG – Telefunken also depended on Zanussi because it was not able to create such production facilities itself in the short run. Zanussi therefore could not be induced to change its policy towards other German buyers by threats of discontinuance or restriction of business relations with AEG – Telefunken. The intended acquisition of a controlling minority share of 25.01 per cent would probably have been prohibited because of its anticompetitive effects on the German market. AEG would have had furthermore the possibility of influencing Zanussi on all its household appliance markets in different countries and thus restrict international competition in this field.

96.   In general, it may be said that the establishement of a joint subsidiary may exclude at least potential competition between parent companies not yet present on the national market concerned.   If at least one of the parent companies has already a business establishment in the market concerned, the degree of concentration will be increased and actual and potential competition will be lessened accordingly. Even if the degree of national concentration is not directly affected, each creation of a joint subsidiary signifies a concentration movement from the international point of view.

97.   One example of the setting up of a joint venture by multinational corporations is the 1967 *Mobay*[405] case.   In this case, the United States Department of Justice took action against Mobay, a joint subsidiary established in 1954 by Monsanto and the German multinational Bayer.   The joint venture had proved to be harmful to competition in the United States because, after its establishment, Monsanto ceased to produce and market flexible polyurethane foam in the United States.   This product was instead exported by Bayer exclusively to Mobay which controlled 50 per cent of the relevant American market.   Having transferred all its shares in Mobay to Bayer in a consent settlement Monsanto was again at least a potential competitor on the relevant market.

5.   *Abusive International Patent Licensing Restrictions.*

(a)   *General Observations*

98.   As already mentioned, patent licensing agreements are frequently used as a vehicle to achieve international market and product allocation, price discrimination and other restrictions both on an individual and a collective basis.   This is partly due to the fact that patent rights generally confer on their holders the exclusive right of exploitation, i.e. a monopoly, and that a number of national legislations tolerate restrictions based on patents but going beyond the scope of the patent rights. Apart from the general difficulties national competition authorities have in controlling the patent licensing policies of multinational enterprises it is frequently almost impossible to assess reliably intra-group licensing practices, as is shown by a United Kingdom study[106], since such practices are in general not embodied in formal agreements.   Of 28 firms covered by the study, only 5 had concluded "formal" agreements within the group.   It is evident that due to the generally informal nature of such arrangements, parent companies may and do regulate the activities of their affiliates by their licensing policy in such a way that it may fall under the competition law of some countries.

99.   In the *Centrafarm* case[107] the European Court of Justice was asked to state whether Article 85 of the EEC Treaty is applicable to a patent licence granted by a parent company to its subsidiary, if the objective of the agreement is to regulate market conditions for licensed products differently between Member states of the EEC.   In the judgement of the Court Article 85 did not apply to agreements between undertakings belonging to the same concern, if the undertakings form an economic unit within which the subsidiary has no real freedom of action and if the agreement was merely concerned with internal allocation of tasks as between undertakings.   The Court, therefore appears to envisage that there may be economic units in which subsidiaries have freedom of action, and in which agreements may have wider effects than organisational arrangements.   It would follow that in such cases the EEC rules of competition may apply even to agreements between parent and subsidiary.   The Commission had made a submission to this effect during the course of the Centrafarm case.

100. The OECD Committee of Experts on Restrictive Business Practices has identified a number of principal types of restrictions frequently operated in connection with patent licensing agreements which subsequently were the object of an OECD Council Recommendation[108]:

- territorial restrictions (e.g. ban on exports and protection of home markets) ;
- use of tied sales ;
- grant-back licensing provisions ;
- package licensing ;
- unjustifiably preventing licensees from competing with third parties ;
- fixing the prices to be charged by licensees.

101. A study by the Spanish Directorate General for Industrial and Technological Development has made available some further information about certain restrictions in licensing agreements. In 1973 the following practices were observed in several hundred licensing contracts with their frequency indicated as a percentage of the total number of contracts examined, including those where no restrictions were found:

1. Export prohibitions   27.3 %
   - global ban   2.3 %
   - prior approval required   5.6 %
   - permitted to specified countries   14.6 %
   - ban to specified countries   4.8 %

2. Restrictions imposed on the exports of the goods   12.8 %
   - obligations to sell to specified enterprises   2.6 %
   - fixing of quotas and maximum exports   0.6 %
   - obligations relating to the use of trademarks   9.0 %
   - other   0.6 %

3. Tied purchases   10.3 %

4. Prohibition on use of non-patented know-how after the contract has
   expired   7.3 %

5. Prohibition on applying other techniques   5.3 %

6. Grant-back obligations   4.0 %

7. Obligations relating to the use of specified trademarks   3.3 %

8. Price controls   2.0 %

102. In *Japan*, the Fair Trade Commission is empowered to examine international agreements involving Japanese firms to ensure that they do not infringe the Anti-Monopoly Act. Where necessary, administrative guidance is given on any restrictive terms in such agreements. The Table on the following page lists the number of agreements reported and a breakdown by various types of restriction of the agreements on which administrative guidance was given over the period 1970-1974.

(b) Individual restrictions

103. A private United Kingdom study[109] on individual patent licensing agreements in the chemical, mechanical and electrical engineering industries found the following restrictions:

30

	Number of enterprises	
Restrictions contained in the licensing agreement	Answering the question	Having such clauses in their licensing agreements
Quantity restrictions	29	8
Market and export restrictions, especially protection of the licensor's home market	29	25
Minimum product prices	29	3
Requirements relating to technical standards (quality etc.)	20	20

In addition, a number of agreements contained restrictions concerning distribution methods, the use of the patented products or the purchase of raw materials.

104. The question whether clauses relating to tied purchases, which, according to the above tables occur rather frequently in patent licensing agreements, restrain competition can only be decided on a case-by-case basis. From the competition point of view, however, such clauses can only be approved if they are necessary for quality control reasons[110]. Examples of tied sales concerning patented or non-patented materials can often be found in the chemical industry[111]. Whereas in the chemical industry the purchase of raw materials is frequently tied, licence agreements in the electrical engineering sector often provide for restrictions concerning the final product, its manufacture or sale[112].

Restrictions in International Contracts Subject to Administrative Guidance in Japan (1970-1974)

Type of Restriction	fiscal Year				
	1970	1971	1972	1973	1974
Unfair business practices	109 (99.1)	113 (100)	282 (100)	590 (100)	504 (99.6)
Restrictions on improved technology	81 (73.6)	71 (62.8)	90 (31.9)	172 (29.2)	159 (31.4)
Restrictions on dealing in competing goods	14 (12.7)	28 (24.8)	67 (23.8)	163 (27.6)	129 (25.5)
Restrictions on sellers supplying licensee with raw materials, parts, etc.	5 (4.5)	4 (3.5)	15 (5.3)	18 (3.1)	32 (6.3)
Imposing of undue prices	4 (3.6)		5 (1.8)	3 (0.5)	3 (0.6)
Restrictions on resale prices	1 (0.9)	7 (6.2)	12 (4.3)	42 (7.1)	31 (6.1)
Quality restrictions	3 (2.7)			6 (1.0)	1 (0.2)
Customer restrictions		1 (0.9)	8 (2.8)	24 (4.1)	14 (2.8)
Suppression of parallel imports			35 (12.4)	65 (11.0)	80 (15.8)
Restrictions of business activity			32 (11.3)	17 (2.9)	26 (5.1)
Restrictions on advertising			9 (3.2)	10 (1.7)	9 (1.8)
Restrictions on sales methods			2 (0.7)	46 (7.8)	6 (1.2)
Other		2 (1.8)	7 (2.5)	24 (4.0)	14 (2.8)
Unreasonable restraints of trade[113]	1 (0.9)				2 (0.4)
Total number of restrictions subject to administrative guidance	110 (100)	113 (100)	282 (100)	590 (100)	506 (100)
The number of contracts which received guidance[114]	110	101	219	497	398
The number of reported international contracts	1.739	4.461	3.117	5.343	6.070
Contrats concerning importation of goods into Japan	1.623	3.860	2.766	4.068	4.276
Contracts on introduction of technology	1.179	1.352	1.409	1.762	1.457
Import agency contracts	41	484	512 (100)	955	701

105. The *German* AEG-Telefunken case may be quoted in this context[115]. The enterprise holding the basic patents for the PAL colour television transmitting and receiving system followed a liberal licensing policy towards manufacturers in countries which opted for this system. Enterprises in countries having adopted a different colour television system were generally granted no licences. This applied in particular to Japan. However, Japanese enterprises succeeded in developing colour television receivers with medium-sized and small screens which, while suited for reception in Germany, do not – in these enterprises' opinion – infringe the relevant patents. The German enterprise thereupon agreed to grant licences also to Japanese enterprises. One Japanese manufacturer felt harmed, however, by the fact that the licence was severely restricted. In particular, the Japanese manufacturers were only allowed to make comparatively small numbers of smaller sets (up to 18 inch screen diagonal) so that the new licensees together were unable to reach a market share exceeding 10 per cent in any country.

106. Unjustified action based on patent rights is sometimes engaged in by multinational enterprises to enforce patents against third parties. Such action may show monopolistic intent which may considerably restrict competition on national as well as on international markets as is illustrated by examples from Spain. There, multinational enterprises and their subsidiaries appear to have exerted considerable pressure on a number of independent small and medium-sized Spanish laboratories by taking or threatening to take legal action against them for imitation or unauthorised use of process and other patents taken out by these companies. As a result of these proceedings or threatened proceedings the Spanish laboratories, because of their smaller financial resources and research facilities, were compelled to discontinue the manufacture and distribution of some of the products, thus leaving these fields to the multinational enterprises.

107. Although basic research is carried out by Government institutions or at least financed by Governments to a significant extent, there are numerous instances of multinational enterprises having managed to acquire individually hundreds or even thousands of patents either through their own research or through buying others' research findings, thus gaining a technological advantage in certain sectors which can hardly be matched by others and which cannot be effectively controlled either by the market or by the competition authorities. A case of a *German* multinational enterprise seeking to justify a merger project by pointing out that this merger was the only possibility to make up for competitive advantages of another multinational enterprise based on a great number of patents held by it, illustrates this situation[116]. In the *United States*, a number of decisions have been taken requiring large multinational firms to grant free licences[117].

(c) Collective Restrictions

108. Cross-licensing agreements which are relatively frequent in certain economic sectors[118] and particularly so where multinational enterprises are present, may affect competition not only by providing for restrictions concerning quantity, price, quality or specific markets but also insofar as enterprises outside the agreement or unable to offer equivalent licences are in a position to make up for the competitive advantage obtained by the pool members only at a very high cost, if at all. A cross-licensing agreement between multinational enterprises in *Germany*, for example, provided that any royalties paid by one of the parties should be lower than those usually payable by third parties. Moreover, these agreements contained clauses or guidelines concerning fixing the prices of the products, the quantities to be produced, the terms of delivery, the in-

dividual markets to be supplied as well as providing for the grant-back of improvements, protection and action against third parties.

109. Although exclusive territorial licences are permitted in some Member countries a restrictive effect of such market sharing can be ascertained. The most quoted example of market sharing by means of a cross-licensing agreement is the 1951 Imperial Chemical Industries case[119]. The case is still of particular interest because it allows the volume of trade during and after the time the restrictions were applied to be compared, thus clearly illustrating the particularly detrimental effect on competition this practice may have. The case involved a cross-licensing agreement between Du Pont and ICI under which the two firms divided the chemical products market between them. Patents were used to limit exports by Du Pont to Great Britain and exports by ICI to the United States. In 1949, ICI's exports to the United States amounted to approximately 500,000 dollars. In 1950, after the removal of the restrictions, the export figure increased tenfold and in the first nine months of 1951 it stood at over 4,000,000 dollars.

110. Restrictions on bulk sales are very frequent in the chemical and drug sectors. They enable multinational firms with patents for manufacturing processes to maintain their control up to the stage of the finished product which is sold to consumers in the form of individual doses at excessive profit. For example, this clause was very recently challenged by the United States Department of Justice in several cases involving international firms. In United States v. Fisons Limited[120], Fisons Pharmaceuticals Limited, a British corporation and subsidiary of Fisons Limited, Colgate-Palmolive Company, a United States corporation, Armour and Company, a United States corporation, and American Home Products Corporation, a United States corporation, were charged, among other things, with market sharing in the distribution and sale of iron dextran for human and veterinary use, with restricting bulk sales of the products, with compelling purchasers of iron dextran to resell under a specified trademark in some cases and under another trademark in other cases. In United States v. Bristol-Myers Company[121] a United States Corporation, a British Corporation, Beecham Group Limited, and Beecham, Inc., a United States firm and subsidiary of Beecham Group Limited, were alleged to have engaged in a combination and conspiracy in unreasonable restraint of trade in ampicillin and other semi-synthetic penicillins. Among other things, it was alleged that licences under patents – including a United States patent issued to Beecham Group Limited – contained clauses restraining the sale semi-synthetic penicillins in bulk form or under other than specified trade names.

111. In the *United States*, the Courts' judgments in 1973 in the case against two Bristish corporations, Glaxo Group Limited and Imperial Chemical Industries (ICI), are particularly illustrative for the anticompetitive effects multinational enterprises have in the field of patent licensing[122]. The judgment terminated the agreements which these corporations had concluded on the manufacture, licensing and marketing of griseofulvin (an anti-fungal agent) in the United States. The corporations had pooled their American patents, the Glaxo Group holding patents for bulk manufacture and packaging of micro-doses while ICI held patents for packaging in dose form. One of the clauses in the agreement was designed to restrict sale and resale at the wholesale stage, while the sub-licensing agreements concluded with American companies prevented the latter from selling griseofulvin in bulk form.

112. In 1970 the United States Department of Justice brought an action which, in view of the size of the firms involved, was of particular importance. The action was brought against the Westinghouse Electric Corporation[123] which is the seventeenth most important firm in the United States in respect of the volume of its sales and two Japanese corporations Mitsubishi Electric and Mitsubishi Heavy Industries, which take eighteenth and thirteenth place respectively among major industrial corporations outside the

United States. The Department of Justice charged that certain agreements between Westinghouse and the two Mitsubishi corporations concerning the exchange of patents and technology licences, and relating to a large number of electrical products, had the effects of preventing sales by the Mitsubishi Corporations of licensed products in the United States and sales by Westinghouse in Japan. Amongst other things, it was charged that the corporations had agreed not to sell licensed products in each other's home country regardless of whether or not such products were patented, and that Westinghouse required the Japanese companies to accept broader licences than they desired, thus extending the territorial restrictions to additional products.

Chapter Two

POSSIBILITIES OF APPLYING RESTRICTIVE BUSINESS PRACTICES LEGISLATION TO THE ACTIVITIES OF MULTINATIONAL ENTERPRISES

I. Introduction

113. The previous chapter of this report has discussed a number of possible and some actually demonstrated competitive problems associated with multinational enterprises. This chapter will discuss the adequacy of national restrictive business practices laws and the relevant regulations in the European Communities for dealing with the actual or potential competitive problems posed by multinational enterprises.

114. One source of difficulty in applying national legislation to multinational enterprises is that such legislation is largely concerned with conduct occuring within national boundaries, while part of the enterprises, information concerning their activities and some or all of their conduct may be outside those boundaries. The gap between antitrust jurisdiction and multinational enterprise activities is not, however, as large as might be supposed. As will be discussed, highly developed antitrust legislation has often been designed and interpreted to apply to transactions occurring partly or even wholly outside the jurisdiction, to treat affiliated or related enterprises as a single unit for purposes of jurisdiction, and to include sanctions for failure to produce relevant information located outside the jurisdiction. This of course does not mean that any present system of legislation is fully adequate to deal with all restrictive business practices which are international in scope. Section III of this chapter will survey in greater detail these provisions as they have been interpreted and applied.

II. Special provisions relating to international restrictive business practices of multinational enterprises

115. Most countries adopt as a principle that the law of competition is of general application and make no distinction between restrictive business practices by multinational and national enterprises. Reference should be made, however, to the 1975 amendments to Canada's Combines Investigation Act which, inter alia, provide remedies where the application in Canada of foreign judgments, laws and directives have anti-competitive effects. Sections 31.5 and 31.6 of the Act empower the Restrictive Trade Practices Commission, upon application by the Director of Investigation and Research, to examine cases where the implementation by any person or company in Canada of foreign judgments, foreign laws, or directives from foreign governments or persons to give effect to a foreign law would:

"*i)* adversely affect competition in Canada.

ii) adversely affect the efficiency of trade or industry in Canada without bringing about or increasing in Canada competition that would restore or improve such efficiency.

iii) adversely affect the foreign trade of Canada without compensating advantages, or

iv) otherwise restrain or injure commerce in Canada without compensating advantages."

In such circumstances to Commission, after hearing hearing the parties concerned, is empowered to issue orders prohibiting or modifying the implementation of such orders, directives, etc. in Canada. Breach of such an order is an offence. Section 31.6 also provides for the issuance of similar orders respecting directives from a person outside Canada who is in a position to influence the policies of a person or company in Canada when the purpose is to give effect to an arrangement which, if entered into in Canada, would have been in violation of section 32 relating to collusive arrangements.

116.   In addition, provision is now made in the Act to deal with the implementation in Canada of collusive arrangements of kinds which, prior to the amendments, might have been beyond the reach of Section 32 because they had been entered into outside Canada by persons in a position to direct or influence the policies of a company in Canada. Section 32 outlaws collusive arrangements which unduly lesson competion. The new provision is in Section 32.1(1) which provides :

" 32.1(1) Any company, wherever incorporated, that carries on business in Canada and that implements, in whole or in part in Canada, a directive, instruction, intimation of policy or other communication to the company or any person from a person in a country other than Canada who is in a position to direct or influence the policies of the company, which communication is for the purpose of giving effect to a conspiracy, combination, agreement or arrangement entered into outside Canada that, if entered into in Canada, would have been in violation of Section 32, is, whether or not any director or officer of the company in Canada has knowledge of the conspiracy, combination, agreement or arrangement, guilty of an indictable offence and is liable on conviction to a fine in the discretion of the court."

117. Where proceedings have been commenced under Section 32.1 no action based substantially on the same facts may be taken by the Director under Section 31.6 relating to foreign laws and directives.

118. In Ireland, Section 12 of the Restrictive Practices Act, 1972, makes special provision for studies and analyses of the operation of multinational enterprises. Section 12 reads as follows:

"In addition to the functions conferred on the Commission by Sections 4, 5, 7 and 9 to 11, the Commission shall study and analyse (and report to the Minister when requested by him the results of any such study or analysis) the effect on the common good of methods of competition, types of restrictive practice, monopolies, the structure of any markets, amalgamation of, or acquisition of, or control of, bodies corporate, the operation of multinational enterprises and relevant legislation, and a study or analysis under this section may either include or consist of a study or analysis of any development outside the State relating to any of the above matters."

III. Application of the legislation on restrictive business practices to the activities of multinational enterprises

1. The criterion of territoriality and the theory of effects

119. An analysis of the territorial scope of laws on restrictive business practices and of the relevant rules adopted in the European Communities reveals that these provisions are applicable to practices in restraint of competition on the domestic market of each country or within the Common Market. However in the United Kingdom, monopoly enquiries can cover exports from the United Kingdom as well as monopoly situations within the national market. The special feature of the United States antitrust laws is that they alone also apply to restrictions on competition which affect the foreign trade of the United States. United States legislation is thus extra-territorial in scope since it governs "commerce... with foreign nations"[124], unlike the legislation of other Member countries which applies only to restrictions on the domestic market, that is, exclusively in the territorial area over which the State exercices its powers. In Sweden and Finland, the law provides for certain possibilities of intervention by the competent authorities when a restriction of competition produces effects outside the national territory. This possibility exists only to the extent necessary for the implementation of conventions or treaties concluded with foreign countries[125]. The territorial scope of laws on restrictive business practices is thus, with the exceptions mentioned, limited to events occurring in the relevant jurisdictions.

120. Besides the definition of the markets to which national law applies, it is also necessary to determine whether the restrictive effects on these markets are sufficient for the purpose of applying national laws (theory of effects) or whether it is not also necessary to require that the acts or behaviour which cause these effects are determined or carried out in whole or in part within the area of national jurisdiction or even that the enterprise which engages in such acts or behaviour is established in this area. In addition, there is the question whether there is anyone within the jurisdiction who can be held responsible. The criterion of effects[126] now appears, to varying extents and degrees discussed herein[127], to be accepted in all Member countries with the exception of the Netherlands, where the explanatory memorandum to the Economic Competition Bill states that concrete acts on Netherlands' territory must take place before the Act can be applied[128], the United Kingdom[129], where legislation explicitly requires a commercial establishment carrying on business in the United Kingdom in addition to restrictive effects, and of Australia, which has adopted a very precise definition of extraterritorial activities which fall within the scope of the legislation[130]. The criterion of effects is embodied in the legislation of Germany[131], Austria[132], Denmark[133], Spain[134], France[135], Sweden[136], and Finland[137]; it has moreover been recognised in the case law of Canada[138], Japan[139], Switzerland[140], the United States[141] and the European Communities[142] and attested by doctrine in Belgium[143].

121. If all the conclusions are drawn from the criterion of effects, as the effects doctrine requires, legislation on restrictive business practices would be applicable to all restrictions on competition having effects on the domestic market and, in the case of the United States, on the domestic market and foreign commerce – in whatever place the acts giving rise to these effects have been committed or decided upon and wherever the enterprise in question may be. In other words, the legislation would apply in the event of a direct, substantial and foreseeable effect on national territory even if enterprises of foreign nationality, having little or no link with the national territory concerned, engage in activities abroad, possibly even by reason of acts not illegal under the foreign law.

122. However, public international law recognises that each State shall determine the scope of applicability of its laws and include within such scope any action taken

abroad, whether or not the authors of such action are its nationals or persons resident on its territory, provided there exists between such acts and its territory a link which reasonably justifies such application. The problem is thus to determine to what extent laws on restrictive business practices are applicable to acts committed abroad which have restrictive effects on national territory and what kind of link between such acts and national territory is necessary to justify such application. As Advocate General Mayras[144] has observed, taking up the ideas outlined in the American Law Institute' s Restatement of the Foreign Relations Law of the United States, the criterion of restrictive territorial effect cannot be accepted as the main criterion of applicability of cartel laws "unless its conditions and its limitations are clarified from the standpoint of public international law". The application of the criterion of restrictive territorial effect, in his view, is subject to three conditions: the restriction of competition on the national market must be direct and immediate, its effect must be reasonably predictable and, finally, there must be a substantial effect. For its part, the Commission of the European Communities referred to an "appreciable effect" within the common market in its Grosfillex/Fillistorf decision.

123. It should however be stressed that the theory of effects which aims at applying to international relations the territorial criterion of antitrust laws has only been applied regularly in the United States, in Germany, in Sweden and in the European Communities. In Switzerland, it has only been applied in one case. The Commission and the Court of Justice of the European Communities have also adopted the theory of effects respectively in the Grosfillex-Fillistorf and Béguelin cases both of which are mentionned below.

124. In the *United States*, case law has confirmed the theory of effects since 1945. It was in regard to one aspect of the case United States v. Aluminium Company of America[145] that the Court for the first time based its conclusion exclusively on the criterion of effects and not on the fact that some of the practices had occurred within the United States. The Alcoa case was also the first case in which the antitrust laws were applied to practices conducted abroad, between foreign enterprises exclusively. Later case law confirmed the principle of effects as described in paragraphs 121 and 122.

125. In *Germany*, some cases involving the application of Section 98(2) of the Act against Restraints of Competition to restrictions originating abroad may be mentioned. Agreements for the auto-limitation of exports concluded by exporters or export associations in Japan in accordance with Sections 5 and 11 respectively of the Japanese Export-Import Trading Act with a view to restricting or co-ordinating the quantities and prices of products sent to the Federal Republic of Germany were drawn up in Japan but had their effects in the Federal Republic of Germany by restricting competition within the meaning of Section 1 of the Act against Restraints of Competition. To that extent, these agreements also fell within the scope of German legislation concerning cartels. Another case involved Scandinavian paper producers who in 1971 concluded agreements concerning prices and conditions of sale of certain categories of paper. These agreements concluded outside the territory of the Federal Republic of Germany made themselves felt on the German market through the selling companies, so that the conditions of Sections 1 and 98(2) of the Act were met and administrative fine proceedings were instituted. In addition, the acquisition of a 49 per cent share in the French limited company Gesparal – a holding company of l'Oréal S.A. – by the Swiss group Nestlé was submitted for examination by the Federal Cartel Office (Section 23 et seq. of the Act) since this acquisition had effects also on the German market notably through the associated companies concerned [Section 98(2) of the Act] and German law was consequently applicable. Finally, the acquisition of Helena Rubinstein by Colgate had an effect on German commerce, notably through the associated companies, so justifying application of German law [Section 98(2) of the Act].

126. In *Sweden*, the Antitrust Act has been applied on several occasions to restrictive business practices from abroad which had effects on the Swedish market[146]. In these cases the foreign firm had a subsidiary, branch office, agent or other representative in Sweden and the antitrust authorities had turned to the firm's representative in Sweden to have a restriction removed. The Antitrust Act is therefore fully applicable to a representative of a foreign firm, i.e. the representative may be convicted of violating the bans on resale price maintenance and collusive tendering and the Market Court may hear the representative with a view to removing any other restraint of trade. In cases of refusal to sell or price discrimination, the Market Court may, on penalty of a fine, enjoin the representative to supply products to firms in Sweden on normal terms. The fact that the representative contends that the restraint of trade is not a consequence of a measure taken by him but stems directly from his principal abroad is not taken into consideration. To illustrate this principle, mention may be made of a Swedish enterprise which was refused supplies of plastic products from British ICI's subsidiary in Sweden. Swedish ICI contended that the decision to withhold supplies had been taken by the British parent company. The Antitrust Ombudsman considered that there was nothing to prevent taking up negociations with Swedish ICI. Following this intervention, supplies were resumed.

127. In *Switzerland*, the Federal Court, in a case concerning a market-sharing agreement based on an exclusive dealing contract between French and Swiss enterprises, considered that it had jurisdiction over the agreement on the grounds that direct effects were produced in Switzerland as alleged by the plaintiff. Although the Act on Cartels and Similar Organisations contains no specific provision in this respect, it is thus recognised that it applies to all restrictive practices which may have direct effects in Switzerland. In this particular case the Federal Court did not pass judgment since it considered it was not competent to do so due to the existence of a bilateral convention on judicial competence in civil legal proceedings[147].

128. The *Commission of the European Communities* has also applied the theory of effects in its decision of 11th March, 1964 in the Grosfillex-Fillistorf case[148]. Grosfillex, a French manufacturer of plastic goods, had appointed the Swiss firm, Fillistorf, as the exclusive distributor of its products in Switzerland and prevented Fillistorf from reselling its goods in the Common Market countries. Since such resale would have meant crossing a new customs frontier, the Commission considered that the restriction of competition resulting from the ban on resale could not have an appreciable effect within the Common Market. In addition, it stated in its notice concerning the importation of Japanese products into the Community[149] that "... the fact that a number or all of the enterprises parties to an agreement have their head offices outside the Community does not affect the applicability of this provision, if the effects of agreements, decisions or concerted practices extend to the territory of the Common Market." Moreover, the Court of Justice of the European Communities appears to have adopted the effects theory in the Béguelin case[150]. The Belgian firm Béguelin and its French subsidiary had each concluded an agreement with the Japanese firm Oshawa under which the latter appointed them the exclusive distributor respectively for Belgium and France of gas pocket lighters bearing the trade mark "Win" manufactured by Oshawa. For Germany, the firm Gebrüder Marbach enjoyed a similar exclusive distributorship. In 1969, the firm G.L. Import Export, of Nice, had imported into France about 18,000 "Win" lighters purchased from Gebrüder Marbach. The Béguelin enterprises asked the French courts to stop these imports on the grounds of unlawful and unfair competition. The defendants argued that the exclusive distribution contract was null and void because it conflicted with Article 85 of the Treaty. The Court's judgment was:

"the fact that one of the enterprises party to the agreement was established in a third country did not prevent this provision from being applied once the agreement produced its effects on the territory of the common market ;

an exclusive dealing agreement between a producer established in a third country and a distributor established in the common market satisfies both the above-mentioned criteria when it constitutes an obstacle, de jure or de facto, to the re-export by the distributor of the products in question to other Member States, or to importation of these products from other Member States into the area covered by the agreement, and to their distribution by persons other than the sole distributor or his customers."

129. In addition, in the conclusions[151] he submitted to the Court of Justice of the European Communities on 2nd May, 1972 in the ICI v. Commission case, Advocate General Mayras, considering the Commission's power to impose fines on firms established outside the Common Market, subscribed to the effects theory. However the Court based its ruling in this case not on the effects theory but on the principle of behaviour or anticompetitive conduct within the Common Market finding that the increases effected in the Common Market concerned competition between producers operating in that market and that the producers established in third countries had determined prices and other conditions of sale which their subsidiaries in the Community were required to apply. The Court therefore held "that, in the circumstances, the formal separation between these companies resulting from their separate legal personalities, did not constitute grounds for denial of their united action on the market so far as application of the laws of competition was concerned." Moreover, the Court found that "by taking advantage of its power of control over its affiliates established within the Community, plaintiff was able to enforce its decision on this market." The Court did not therefore deliver judgment on the question whether, in order to apply the rules of competition to enterprises established in third countries, it was sufficient that the enterprises should bring about certain effects within the Common Market by means of restrictions on competition which were committed outside the Common Market[152].

2. Theory of enterprise unity or agency

130. The theory of effects is the basis of legislation, jurisprudence and administrative practices which establish the authority of individual Member countries and of the European Communities to judge the restrictive or abusive effects emanating from outside and felt within the relevant territory. The theory of enterprise unity is to some extent complementary to the theory of effects and is of particular importance in relation to multinational enterprises with many establishments. The theory of enterprise unity involves considering as a single economic entity, and even though they have separate legal personalities, enterprises belonging to the same group and subject to the same control, such as groups composed of parent company and subsidiaries. In a number of cases in the field of competition law it has been possible to ascribe the restrictive behaviour of the subsidiary or parent located abroad to the parent or subsidiary located on national territory. The concept of enterprise unity thus allows the question of responsability to be settled as well as enabling solutions to be found to problems of investigation, service of process and enforcement in cases involving foreign enterprises: these problems will be examined in more detail in the following section. This concept of enterprise unity may also be found in a number of proposed or new company laws. For example, German legislation provides that within a Konzern the parent company is jointly responsible with the subsidiary for the latter's activities.

131. Though it is complementary to the theory of effects the theory of enterprise unity may be considered of intrinsic value in legislations or case law requiring proof of behaviour occurring within the territory concerned. This may be the case in particular if there is the requirement of a commercial establishment (United Kingdom legislation)

40

or if there is a subsidiary under the control of a foreign-based parent. The theory of enterprise unity is thus to be understood as an example of the application of the behaviour principle but should not lead to automatically imputing the subsidiary's behaviour to the parent nor to denial of any independence of action on the part of the subsidiaries which have been established with distinct legal personalities under the various companies laws in force in the countries in which they operate. For instance, reference to cases involving multinational enterprises which have arisen under Articles 85 and 86 of the Treaty of Rome shows that the Court of Justice of the European Communities has almost always laid special emphasis on the intervention of the foreign parent company within the Common Market by means of or in agreement with its subsidiary established there. It has only had recourse to the theory of enterprise unity essentially in order to establish the Commission's competence to take action against the parent company established in a third country.

132. The *Commission of the European Communities* recognised the special circumstances of members of a group when it issued a negative clearance on 18th June, 1969 for an agreement between a Danish parent company and its Dutch subsidiary on the grounds that the two enterprises were not in competition with each other since the agreement was an internal allocation of tasks, the subsidiary being considered by the Commission as an integral part of the economic entity constituted by the Christiani and Nielsen international group[153]. In the dyestuffs case[154], Article 85 of the Rome Treaty was applied to the parent companies. The Court considered that these companies had acted directly within the Common Market through the intermediary of subsidiaries who acted as agents for their parent companies and the latter were therefore held to be responsible for the actions of their subsidiaries which they had inspired. In the Zoja/CSC case[155] the Court of Justice applied the same principle in a case involving Article 86 of the Treaty.

133. In *Germany* , although no case of this kind has been decided by the Federal Cartel Office or by the Courts, it appears that the parent company established in Germany can be held responsible for the restrictive behaviour of a subsidiary established abroad but only to the extent that the restrictive effects are felt on the German market and in cases where a person authorised to represent the parent company has caused such behaviour or failed to fulfil his supervisory duty. If a nationally based subsidiary engages in restrictive business practices as a result of the instructions it has received from its foreign parent, it may also be punished by a fine in addition to a fine on the members of the Board of Management authorised to represent it. On the other hand, if the restrictive behaviour which has an effect in Germany is caused by the foreign parent without the participation of the subsidiary established in Germany, the national subsidiary cannot be held responsible. However in the case of a wholly owned German subsidiary, a fine may be levied on its property since the group is in principle considered to be a single economic entity. Difficulties are likely to arise when the subsidiary is less than 100 per cent owned by one foreign parent for, in this case, enforcement of the fine would affect property belonging to third parties who might not have participated in the restrictive behaviour.

134. In *Sweden*, if a foreign subsidiary of a Swedish parent engages in a restraint of trade affecting the Swedish market the legislation provides that proceedings and where appropriate remedial action may be taken against the Swedish parent on the doctrine of enterprise unity.

135. In *Switzerland*, action cannot be taken against the Swiss subsidiary of a foreign based parent unless it has participated in the restriction of competition. However, the authorities have not yet had to decide this question.

136. In the *United Kingdom,* jurisdiction cannot be established under the Restrictive Trade Practices Acts over a foreign corporation simply because it has a parent or subsidiary in the United Kingdom. However, while U.K. monopoly legislation is concerned with monopoly situations in the United Kingdom, it has proved possible to exercise some influence over a multinational and its behaviour by controlling the domestic subsidiary where this subsidiary is a monopolist. For example in the Hoffman-La Roche case the excessive transfer prices of the multinational to the domestic subsidiary were taken into account by the Monopolies Commission in determining whether excessive profits were being made in connection with the supply of Librium and Valium in the United Kingdom. But there can be no direct exercice of jurisdiction over the overseas parent through the domestic subsidiary [see section 90 (3) of the Fair Trading Act].

137. In the *United States,* the courts have frequently held domestic parent companies of multinational enterprises accountable for the restrictive behaviour of their foreign subsidiaries, provided, of course, that such restrictive behaviour constitutes a violation of the U. S. law. For instance, in Continental Ore Co. v. Union Carbide & Carbon Co.[156] the Supreme Court held Union Carbide & Carbon chargeable with an attempt to monopolise the vanadium market through certain activities of its Canadian subsidiary. Also the Federal Trade Commission, in the Matter of Litton Industries[157], held the domestic parent company responsible for a potential elimination of competition between itself and foreign typewriter manufacturing concerns which it had acquired. The Federal Trade Commission recently denounced, in the Matter of Xerox Corporation,[158] the activities of foreign subsidiaries of Xerox, including Rank Xerox and Fuji Xerox, as well as the domestic parent company. A consent agreement settling the matter was accepted during July 1975.

138. The proposition of holding United States subsidiaries accountable for the behaviour of their foreign parent companies presupposes again, first, that the restrictive behaviour of the parent abroad constitutes a substantive violation of U.S. antitrust law. Secondly, it presupposes that the United States subsidiary participated in some measure in the parent's restrictive scheme. Since the foreign parent's behaviour is a violation of U.S. law only if it is effective or intended to be effective in the United States, its U.S. subsidiary will almost certainly have participated in putting the scheme across. Examples of cases in which U.S. subsidiaries were charged with restrictive behaviour of their foreign parent companies are United States v. Ciba Corporation[159], charging the U.S. subsidiary along with its foreign parent and United States v. Bristol-Myers Co. et al.[160], charging, among other defendants, Beecham Group Limited, England, and its U.S. subsidiary, Beecham Inc.

139. In the United States the proposition of charging a U.S. subsidiary of a foreign parent with the parent's antitrust violation may be of less practical significance than in some other countries. The extraterritorial reach of U.S. antitrust law which is recognised by U.S. courts makes it frequently possible to prosecute the foreign parent companies, including foreign multinational companies, directly, and in their own name. This was done, for example, in United States v. Watchmakers of Switzerland Information Center, Inc.[161] and in United States v. Imperial Chemical Industries Ltd.[162]. In such cases the difficulty sometimes is to establish contacts jurisdiction[163] and to effect proper service of process. In general, the test for determining whether personal jurisdiction may be established and service of process may be effectuated in a criminal proceeding is whether the enterprise or an appropriate agent is found within the United States and whether service on an appropriate agent has been effected. The test in a civil proceeding is simple ; if the enterprise or its appropriate agent is found or transacts business within the United States service may be made by mail abroad and/or appointment of an agent for service of process abroad. United States courts have been in-

creasingly expansive in holding that relatively limited business contacts with United States markets may constitute transacting business within the United States. This problem is more fully discussed below, paragraphs 163 to 169.

140. In *Canada*, elements of the concept of enterprise unity are to be found in certain provisions of the Combines Investigation Act, some of which are referred to in Section II above.

IV. Issues in applying legislation on restrictive business practices to the activities of multinational enterprises

141. Since the legislation of most Member countries applies, in principle, to all practices the effects of which are felt on the national territory, whether a national or a foreign company is responsible, there is therefore no difficulty, in principle, from the point of view of substantive law, in applying legislation to these practices. From the point of view of procedure, on the other hand, the fact that multinational enterprises are involved may give rise to complications with regard to jurisdiction to the extent that it proves necessary to apply the law extraterritorially. Thus, although international law allows a State to extend its jurisdiction to acts committed abroad (juridictio) on condition that such acts produce effects within its frontiers, it cannot exercise its jurisdiction (imperium) outside its frontiers and in particular use its powers of investigation, command and enforcement without coming into conflict with the sovereign power of other States on their own territories. This disjunction between jurisdiction and its exercise raises problems for Member countries in their relations with multinational enterprises, notably as concerns the communication of procedural documents, the collection of evidence and the enforcement of decisions. In addition, to the extent that the exercice of jurisdiction concerns a foreign enterprise, as would be the case for example with the extraterritorial application of restrictive business practices legislation, such action concerns not only the relationship between the country exercising its jurisdiction and the enterprise involved but also the relationship between that country and the other country in which the enterprise in question is established.

142. The proper limits to be assigned to the extraterritorial application of laws on restrictive business practices have been among the subjects to which international public law specialists have given particular attention and which have often been discussed at international conferences. Without examining in detail the various theories and opinions on this question, it seems worthwhile to mention the work of the American Law Institute and the International Law Association in this field. In item 2(d) of the Restatement of the Foreign Relations Law of the United States, Section 40 (1965), the American Law Institute suggested the following considerations as to comity:

> "Where two states have jurisdiction to prescribe and enforce rules of law and the rules they may prescribe require inconsistent conduct upon the part of a person, each state is required by international law to consider, in good faith, moderating the exercice of its enforcement jurisdiction, in the light of such factors as
>
> *(a)* vital national interests of each of the states,
> *(b)* the extent and the nature of the hardship that inconsistent enforcement actions would impose upon the person,
> *(c)* the extent to which the required conduct is to take place in the territory of the other state,
> *(d)* the extent to which enforcement by action of either state can reasonably

be expected to achieve compliance with the rule prescribed by that state."

The Court of Appeals for the Second Circuit in a Justice Department antitrust grand jury proceeding involving obtaining documents from Germany[164] quoted and generally followed these guidelines.

143. The International Law Association, at its 55th conference in New York in August 1972 , also approved principles for the solution of problems concerning the assumption and exercice of jurisdiction by States in connection with restrictive trade practices. Article 7 of the ILA Resolution reads:

> "In the event of there being concurrent jurisdiction of two or more States so as to create a conflict with respect to the conduct of any person:
>
> *(a)* no State shall require conduct within the territory of another State which is contrary to the law of the latter, and
>
> *(b)* each State shall, in applying its own law to conduct in another State, pay due respect to the major interests and economic policies of such other State."

1. *Problems in obtaining information about the restrictive business practices of multinational enterprises*

144. A problem in evaluating the conduct of multinational enterprises is the varying amount and quality of obtainable information on their activities. These difficulties manifest themselves in two different respects: the first concerns the collection of general data on the size and scope of foreign investment – for example, sales, purchases and market shares in relevant product and geographic markets[165] [for further discussion of this problem see paragraphs 13 to 21]. Much of this information may be quite relevant to the enforcement of competition policy in relation to multinational enterprises. Apart from information gathered in enforcing restrictive business practices laws, other useful kinds of information from a competition viewpoint might be derived from foreign investment and takeover regulations since the latter allow a general picture to be drawn of the extent and direction of foreign investment. On the other hand, it should be stressed that countries which have adopted such laws have done so for a variety of economic and political reasons so that most of the information gathered under such laws is only of limited interest to the competition authorities. There are also other methods allowing the collection of some basic data on the operations of multinational enterprises as well as of purely domestic enterprises, the most significant being exchange control laws and regulations for inward and outward investment, companies and corporations acts, taxation and general statistical laws which require the firms to disclose some details of their operations.

145. However, information gathered is usually of limited significance for the enforcement of competition laws which require detailed information on the behaviour of individual firms and the structure of individual markets. Moreover much of the information gathered under existing laws is obtained for the specific purpose of the law in question and is subject to secrecy rules. On this account, except where aggregated information is published, such information cannot be communicated to other persons not members of the government departments responsible for collecting it[166]. However, the question may be raised whether the information that is available and can be disclosed , bearing in mind the necessary secrecy provisions , can be better co-ordinated and communicated between different departments responsible for enforcing the different regulations. It is a fact that many agencies are responsible for monitoring the various aspects of direct investment so that a detailed overall assessment of its impact on industry

structure and performance such as is sometimes required in determining the possible existence of restrictive practices is made difficult. In Germany, for example, under the Concentration Act the Federal Office for Trade and Industry is empowered to investigate the development of concentration within the Federal Republic but is expressly forbidden to pass on the information collected to the competition authorities.

146. The second set of difficulties arises in the context of applying restrictive business practices legislation. More specific methods designed to obtain information on the behaviour of individual firms (whether multinational or not) are available to the competition authorities in most Member countries. These most often take the form of compulsory notification and registration procedures for different types of restrictive agreements, mergers and monopolies and general powers conferred upon the authorities to undertake enquiries and to bring actions in the application of restrictive business practices legislation.

147. When applying these general powers however in the case of multinational enterprises, the authorities in many Member countries have sometimes been faced with a number of problems in the collection of relevant information. Again, two main types of problem may be distinguished: first of all, difficulties have arisen in obtaining all or most of the relevant documents which the competition authorities require for the investigation or prosecution of a particular restrictive business practices case. The documents involved here are written agreements, letters, memoranda, etc. which may not be in the hands of the nationally-based subsidiary or parent of a multinational enterprise subject to the jurisdiction of the national authority but which are in certain cases only obtainable from a foreign-based branch or a firm beyond the reach of national laws, except when the branches voluntarily submit such information ; the second type of information frequently needed to assess the reasonableness of certain practices concerns such details as costs, prices and profits of the multinational group as a whole in its different product and geographical markets. Information of this kind is especially useful to authorities responsible for applying legislation based on the criterion of abuse since, without full information, they may be unable to be totally accurate in distinguishing those of the measures taken by a multinational enterprise which may be justified on economic grounds and those which constitute abuse or discrimination.

(a) *Problems resulting from the multinational nature of the enterprise*

148. Despite the possibilities of obtaining information under restrictive business practices laws from any domestically-based affiliate of a multinational enterprise several Member countries have encountered difficulties in obtaining some information considered relevant to a restrictive business practices case which is only available from a subsidiary or parent established abroad and consequently outside the area in which the competent authorities may exercise jurisdiction. In the case of a multinational enterprise without a head office, official representative or property on national territory, it is difficult not only to obtain evidence, as mentionned above, but also to serve procedural documents, in particular, requests or orders for information (see paragraph 162 et seq.).

149. Even when the multinational had a legal representative on national territory, several Member countries reported difficulties in obtaining data. This problem arises most acutely when only a subsidiary is located on national territory, less so when the parent is home based. Thus in *Sweden,* when the parent company is located on national territory it may under certain conditions be ordered, on the basis of the Investigation Act, to produce data available not only on its own premises but also on the premises of its subsidiary located abroad. It is also possible to demand the presence

of the parent company at hearings to give an explanation about a restriction of competition practised by its foreign subsidiary on the Swedish market. On the other hand, when only a subsidiary of a foreign enterprise is established in Sweden, the authorities may have problems trying to procure material that is required to make an assessment if this material is available only from the parent company. Foreign companies have, in certain cases, voluntarily released information to the antitrust authorities. The Investigation Act has as yet not been invoked to compel the subsidiary to furnish data which are available only on the premises of the foreign parent company.

150.   In *Denmark*, the Monopolies Control Authority experienced difficulties in assessing the reasonableness of the invoice price of crude oil and petroleum products paid by Danish subsidiaries to their foreign parent companies since the Authority could not gain access to the parent companies' methods of calculating the invoice prices, including profit margins.

151.   In *Germany*, in the proceedings against the international oil companies (see paragraph 72 above) the Federal Cartel Office was unable to obtain from the nationally-based subsidiaries information on the cost of crude oil necessary for determining the reasonableness of the prices paid by the subsidiaries to their foreign parents, the subsidiaries in turn being unable to obtain such information from their parent companies. Also in merger cases involving multinational enterprises, German subsidiaries have met with considerable problems when asked to supply information on the group's activities as a whole as required under Sections 23 and 24 of the Act against Restraints of Competition.

152.   Although this did not prevent effective action being taken, a similar difficulty was encountered by the *United Kingdom* Monopolies and Mergers Commission in its investigation of the supply of chlordiazepoxide and diazepam. The Commission's principal concern was with the costs of and profits from the sale of Librium and Valium incurred by the Roche multinational group and the group refused to supply certain information mainly concerning the world-wide sales of the two drugs which the Commission considered necessary to justify the group's claims as to the proper charge for research expenditure.

153.   Another problem of information which has occurred in a few U.S. court cases concerns the situation where a party to an antitrust proceeding has claimed that a document located in a foreign country was privileged on grounds of sovereignty. In re Investigation of World Arrangements[167] the oil companies subpoenaed objected on the ground that documents within the territory of a foreign sovereign were privileged. The court held that this privilege belongs solely to the foreign sovereign « and it cannot be claimed by a party for his own benefit, particularly so when the party is not a national of the sovereign involved ». Moreover, the court reserved judgment on the validity of such a claim of privilege even if advanced directly by a foreign government. The companies subpoenaed also objected on the ground that the laws of some foreign countries prohibited the removal of papers from within their territorial jurisdictions. The court ruled that "calling for the disclosure of documents is a procedural matter and it has long been the rule that the "lex fori' governs the law of procedure." However, the court did not "particularly desire" to promulgate a procedural order that imposed serious criminal penalties under foreign substantive law. Accordingly the court reserved judgement pending the companies showing good faith in trying to secure the consent of foreign sovereigns to remove required documents or copies, or refusal by the foreign sovereign.

154.   The preceding paragraphs have shown that there appear to be some variations between countries with regard to the degree of difficulty in obtaining information from

multinational enterprises depending on whether the national branch of the multinational is the parent or a subsidiary. When the multinational enterprise does not have an establishment on national territory, in general Member countries have not attempted to use compulsory means to obtain the information needed in a particular case. When the parent company is established on national territory most countries, following the example of Sweden, appear to consider that it is relatively simple to obtain information from the parent, sometimes even about the behaviour of their subsidiaries located abroad. On the other hand, if the subsidiary is established on national territory and the parent company abroad, most Member countries consider that it is more difficult to obtain information by compulsory process and they generally do not attempt to obtain it. However, this is not the case in Germany where (as indicated in paragraph 176 below) requests for information may be addressed to the parent multinational established abroad and served on the domestic subsidiary subject to an administrative fine in the event of the latter's failure to produce the information. Moreover, if the enterprise does not supply the information requested, the burden of proof may be reversed or merger notifications may be considered incomplete. In the United States, the courts have on several occasions ordered the production of documents located abroad in the foreign parent or subsidiary. As shown in the cases described below, refusal to produce documents, if it results from the bad faith of the enterprise however much concealed by foreign legal prohibitions on the disclosure of information may give rise to the imposition of fines or be interpreted unfavourably in relation to be the multinational enterprise.

(b) *Obstacles to the disclosure of information abroad originating in the laws or regulations of some Member countries*

155. There are three main obstacles to the disclosure of information to foreign authorities. The first results from the general prohibition on the disclosure by both national authorities and private enterprises of State, manufacturing or business secrets or of any other kind of information obtained for specific purposes, for example, under competition, fiscal or companies' legislation. These prohibitions apply equally to disclosure to other national or to foreign antitrust authorities.

156. The second obstacle stems from secrecy obligations upon national authorities when receiving information from enterprises on a voluntary basis. Disclosure to foreign authorities of information obtained in this way or putting it to a use other than that intended could amount to an abuse of the good faith of the enterprise supplying it for a specific purpose. For this reason, this type of voluntary information is not normally disclosed except with the consent of the enterprise concerned. Indeed, if this were otherwise, all sources of voluntary information would rapidly dry up. In this connection it is worth noting that the United Kingdom is the only Member country to rely essentially on the voluntary procedure for collecting information. Other Member countries rarely use this approach and when they do, it is in the absence of other means. In the United States, unless express assurances of secrecy have been given by the antitrust enforcement authorities, there is no obstacle to the disclosure by them of information voluntarily submitted. Further, the breadth of the recent amendments to the Freedom of Information Act in the United States have raised serious questions about the ability of government agencies to keep such information secret even in cases where express assurances have been given. In addition, there is nothing to prevent enterprises, except in the case of a legal prohibition or government order to the contrary, from supplying information to foreign antitrust authorities voluntarily. In many cases multinational enterprises have spontaneously replied to requests of this kind.

157. The third obstacle concerns prohibitions on the disclosure of documents abroad, including documents of relevance in the antitrust field. These prohibitions may appear in the law itself or they may take the form of a specific government order prohibiting enterprises from disclosing to foreign authorities information on their activities as a result of an antitrust action abroad. For example, Section 39 of the Netherlands' Economic Competition Act prohibits Dutch enterprises from disclosing documents and from complying with any measures or decisions taken by any other State relating to any regulations of competition, dominant positions or conduct restricting competition, unless special exceptions or exemptions are granted. In addition, two Canadian provinces – Ontario and Quebec – prohibit removal of business records that may be in compliance with orders issued outside provincial jurisdiction. In the United Kingdom, the Shipping Contracts and Commercial Documents Act 1964 provides that where a foreign court or authority require the disclosure of a commercial document not within the territorial jurisdiction of the foreign country, and the requirement constitutes an infringement of the jurisdiction which, under international law, belongs to the United Kingdom, a United Kingdom Minister may direct the United Kingdom company or person not to comply with the requirement. Similar provisions to the United Kingdom Act have been adopted in several other Member countries concerning the shipping industry – Belgium, Denmark, Finland, France, Germany, Norway and Sweden – designed to prohibit ship-owners from submitting information to foreign authorities except with special government permission.

158. In practice, it has been as a consequence of antitrust proceedings in the United States that some governments have forbidden their nationals, including U.S. subsidiaries in their country, from responding to a United States request or demand for documents[168]. There have been at least eight instances of antitrust proceedings (Grand Jury Investigations and court cases) in which United States Courts were asked to enforce subpoenas against enterprises which were nationals of foreign jurisdictions with regulations prohibiting such disclosure. United States Courts have, in these cases, applied the principles of comity as set forth in paragraph 142, supra, as they relate to the specific facts before them. The results in these cases are not easily summarised in a single principle. Nevertheless, they indicate judicial willingness to enforce subpoenas, notwithstanding contrary foreign law, where the foreign national has failed to make a convincing showing that it has undertaken a good faith effort to have its government waive or suspend the enforcement of the contrary law in the particular case.

159. In the *United States*, documents of foreign affiliates of United States companies are generally subject to production orders issuing from United States Federal Courts if the foreign affiliate is controlled and managed by the American company. United States v. First National City Bank[169] illustrates this point. In that case, the German division of First National City Bank of New York was subpoened to produce documents located in Germany relating to transactions of one of its customers. The defendant argued that to produce the documents would give rise to civil liability in Germany for "divulging information relating to the affairs of its customers"[170]. The court, in rejecting defendant's argument, stated that the test for orders to produce foreign documents required the court to "balance the national interests of the United States and Germany and to give appropriate weight to the hardship, if any... [defendant would] ... suffer"[171]. Citing examples under which that test would militate in favour of non-production of documents, such as violations of foreign criminal law or its equivalent, or conflict with legislation of a foreign power, the court found that the United States' interest in enforcing its antitrust laws, "... considered the cornerstones of ... [that] ... nation's economic policies",[172] outweighed the interests of Germany and any hardships that might ensue to defendant. Therefore, the German division of First City was required to produce its document[173].

160. In another case involving a U.K. company, Beecham Group Ltd. [in re Ampicillin Antitrust Litigation, M.D.C., Docket N° 50, Civ. N° 822-70 (D.D.C.)], Beecham failed to comply with a discovery order. In its defence, Beecham presented an order of the U.K. Department of Trade and Industry which prohibited the production. The Court found that Beecham had not taken all affirmative steps, such as a petition for reconsideration or negotiation, required to achieve compliance with the Court's discovery orders. Accordingly, the court ruled that the facts warranted the application of the negative-resolution-of-facts sanction under Rule 37(b) of the Federal Rules of Civil Procedure. Briefly, this provides that when a person fails to obey an order to provide discovery, the facts in question shall be taken to be established. Subsequently the British Government relented and allowed production of all but thirty-five documents relating to confidential relations between Beecham and the British Government. Several thousand documents were produced to the general satisfaction of the Justice Department. Thereafter, the Court vacated the negative-resolution-of-facts order.

161. These last cases also illustrate the point that although the existence of legal provisions in other countries may be an obstacle in some cases to the investigation or prosecution of a restrictive business practice, national courts and authorities are not powerless in all cases to obtain documents located abroad. Failure to produce documents not privileged or subject to special regulations has sometimes been interpreted by such bodies unfavourably to the multinational enterprises involved and even when foreign laws are invoked as a justification for not producing particular documents national courts may require the enterprises concerned to demonstrate that they have made an effort to comply with the national court's ruling.

2. *Problems concerning the establishment of bases for jurisdiction and effecting the service of procedural documents*

162. It appears that Member countries whose legislation is founded on the principle of abuse do not often apply their laws to restrictive business practices originating abroad when there is no enterprise within the jurisdiction on which to serve process or when there are great difficulties in obtaining the information necessary to determine the existence of an abuse or to determine the harmful effects on the public interest. Among Member countries recognising the criterion of effects on national territory, Canada is the only country that, on the basis of its jurisprudence, has refrained from applying its legislation if the parties involved cannot be served in Canada.

163. In the *United States*, cases involving foreign persons or companies generally raise a delicate problem of personal jurisdiction. In cases of this kind a determination must be made whether the foreign companies are engaged in business activities in the United States to such an extent as to justify the jurisdiction of a United States court. Section 12 of the Clayton Act is the basic provision governing *in personam* jurisdiction in antitrust litigation. Its function is to fix the venue, or place of suit in antitrust cases, and determine where defendant may be served with process in such suits. Section 12 provides that "any suit, action, or proceeding under the antitrust laws against a corporation may be brought... in a judicial district wherein it may be found or transacts business." Service of process under Section 12 may be accomplished wherever the defendant may be "found".

164. The leading Supreme Court case involving the application of Section 12 to foreign defendants is United States v. Scophony Corp[174]. The Court in that case held that defendant was "transacting business" and was "found" in the Southern District of New York, within the meaning of Section 12 of the Clayton Act, and therefore was subject to being sued and served there for violations of the Sherman Act[175]. The case in-

volved efforts by a British corporation to exploit its television patents and inventions in the United States through a number of arrangements with American corporations. The British company was constantly involved in supervising the United States arrangements and was represented in the United States by two of its directors, one of whom had a comprehensive power of attorney to protect the company's United States interests. The Court in interpreting the venue provision in Section 12 found the term "transacting business" to mean "The practical, everyday business or commercial concept of doing or carrying on business of any substantial character..."[176].

165. In the Swiss Watchmakers case[177], which also involved the issue of service of process on foreign defendants under Section 12 of the Clayton Act, the court held the foreign defendants could be "found" in the United States through the activities of their American subsidiary. Noting that the American subsidiary had no independent business activities of its own the court deemed the Swiss parents "found" in the United States and thus properly served in the Southern District of New York.

166. Service of process under Section 12 of the Clayton Act is not restricted to the territorial limits of the United States. In Hoffman Motors Corp. v. Alfa Romeo[178] the foreign defendants argued that Section 12 of the Clayton Act barred service outside the United States because that section required service "in any judicial district in which the defendant may be "found". The court rejected this argument and held that defendant could be served wherever it was "found", including outside the United States as long as defendant had certain "minimal" contacts with the jurisdiction out of which process... (was)... issued". In addition to Section 12 of the Clayton Act, Rule 4 of the Federal Rules of Civil Procedure may also be used to perfect service of process on foreign defendants. Rule 4 permits "a party not an inhabitant of the state or found... (therein)... to be served with process in a federal court in the manner and under the circumstances prescribed by a state statute". This allows the federal courts to use state "long arm" statutes for service of process on foreign defendants for violations of American antitrust laws arising out of the defendants' activities within the state. In the Hoffman Motors case Rule 4 was applied and the defendant properly served in Italy by registered mail and by personal service on the Italian company's general manager by a court-appointed Italian attorney.

167. Service of process in certain antitrust cases has also been held valid under 35 U.S.C. paragraph 293. Under this section the non-resident patentee may designate a resident agent in the United States for service of process. In the absence of such designation, "the United States District Court for the District of Columbia shall have jurisdiction and summons shall be served by publication or otherwise as the court directs." In United States v. Farbenfabriken Bayer A.G.[179], an antitrust case involving use restrictions under patent licensing, Bayer was served by registered mail in Germany and the district court held that Bayer was properly served.

168. Despite the cases just quoted the problem of personal jurisdiction often remains difficult to solve. The Government recognised this in United States v. N.V. Nederlandsche Combinatie Voor Chemische Industrie, et al.[180] in which it accepted the plea of nolo contendere by the Dutch corporation "because, among other considerations, the question of jurisdiction over said defendant presents serious problems which could probably be resolved only after protracted litigation and subsequent appeal".

169. The conclusion to be drawn from these cases is that each case raises special problems and that before bringing an action, the Department of Justice must consider the possibility that the foreign defendant will challenge the court's contacts jurisdiction over him[181]. Once the court decides it has jurisdiction in the face of a foreign defendant's challenge (as in United States v. Farbenfabriken Bayer A.G. and Chemagro

Corp., Civ. N° 586-68), or once the foreign corporation voluntarily submits to the court's jurisduction (as in United States v. Westinghouse Electric Corporation et al., Civ. N° C 70-852-SAW)problems arising from the multinational character of the defendant are very much minimised. Where the alleged restrictive business practice can be effectively enjoined by action against the United States component corporation only – whether that component be a United States subsidiary of a foreign parent, as in United States v. CIBA Corporation[182], or the United States parent company, as in United States v. The Gillette Company[183], there are no special problems relating to personal jurisdiction arising from the multinational nature of the enterprise.

170. In the *European Communities*, the communication of procedural documents to the enterprises concerned, in particular the statement of objections and the notification of decisions, does not seem to have given rise to any major difficulties. However the Commission cannot be certain that in some future case the communication of procedural documents will not raise problems with regard to multinational companies whose centre of decision is outside the Community.

171. It should be noted that the Court of Justice has adopted a very pragmatic attitude towards these questions which is designed to facilitate considerably the procedural formalities. As regards the statement of objections, the Court rejected, in its Geigy and Sandoz judgments[184], the enterprises' request for annulment of the Commission's decision, the enterprises claiming that the Commission had communicated the statement of objections in a manner which was not in conformity with the Swiss law under which this communiction should have been made (Switzerland not recognising the validity on its territory of delivery through the post of foreign legal documents of this type).

172. The Court based its judgment on the following reasons :

"whereas, since there is no convention between the Communities and the Swiss Confederation on the subject, notice given to parties established outside the Community is subject to international practice and must be in a form to take into account the jurisdiction of both the Community and the third State involved ;

whereas the documents indicate that the authorities of the third State concerned do not at the present time recognise that there is any way in practice to give notice in the territory of that State in a manner that they consider valid under national law ;

hence, international law cannot be invoked to deny the Community the power to take the necessary steps to ensure the effectiveness of measures against acts impairing competition that take place within the Common Market, even where the perpetrator of these acts is established in a third country ;

in addition, the primary purpose of the statement of objections is to ensure that the parties are able to exercise their rights under the Treaty and Community legislation ;

in these circumstances, notice given in conformity with Community regulations cannot result in the invalidity of the ensuing administrative proceedings because of the fact that it must be effected in a third country so long as it makes it possible for the recipient effectively to know what the objections raised against him are, thereby fulfilling its purpose ;".

173. As concerns the notification of the decisions to the ICI, Geigy and Sandoz companies, the Court in its ICI judgment[185] rejected the claim that the fact that the Commission had notified its decision to the registered office of the appellant's subsidiaries established in the Common Market, violated the Treaty or, at least, essential procedural requirements. The Court also rejected the argument that the German subsidiary of ICI, to which notification of the Decision was made by the Commission, had received no mandate from the parent company to receive notification and was not obliged under

German law to bring the documents in question to the notice of the parent company. The Court held that irregularities in the procedure of notification of a decision were external to the legal act and could therefore not vitiate it.

174. In the Continental Can[186] judgment, the Court stated its position as follows :

> "The undertaking had received one or two letters from the Commission by post in December 1971, although the decision should have been notified through diplomatic channels.
> A decision is properly notified within the meaning of the Treaty, if it reaches the addressee and puts the latter in a position to take cognizance of it. This was so in the present case, because the contested decision actually reached Continental and the latter cannot make use of its own refusal to take cognizance of the decision in order to render this communication ineffective."

175. In *Japan*, the service of procedural documents raises many difficulties. Section 50 (2) of the Antimonopoly Act provides that the formal hearing procedure shall be commenced by serving a certified copy of the complaint upon the respondent. Section 69-2 of the Act provides that the provisions of Sections 162, 169, 171 and 177 of the Code of Civil Procedure shall apply mutatis mutandis with regard to the service of documents. But neither Section 175 of the Code, providing for the service of documents in a foreign country, nor Section 178 of the Code, providing for the service of documents by public notification, are mentioned. The lack of such provisions has raised difficulties in commencing the hearing procedure against foreign companies. One instance of such difficulty was the Nippon Yusen Kaisha case[187] when the Fair Trade Commission withdrew their complaint against 10 foreign entrepreneurs operating their businesses through agents in Japan. The 10 entrepreneurs insisted that the agents, on which the FTC had served the certified copy, had no right to receive it, and if they had received it in fact, the receipt could not be valid without ratification by the representatives of the respondents.

176. The situation in *Germany* provides a good illustration of how the problem of service of procedural documents abroad is closely linked with the collection of information necessary for investigating a case. According to Section 46 of the Act against Restraints of Competition the Federal Cartel Office may, in connection with a particular case, request information from an enterprise, regardless of whether the registered office of the enterprise to which the request for information is directed is located in Germany or abroad. Such acts de iure imperio in the shape of a decision requesting information are not in contradiction with the international law principle of the territoriality of acts de iure imperio ; for this only forbids the ordering or enforcement of acts de iure imperio abroad, but does not restrict its power to issue orders to foreign-based parent companies of multinational enterprises on account of their practices which have an effect inside Germany. In German court practice, too, such requests for information are, in principle, considered admissible[188]. If the enterprise fails to provide the necessary records, the onus of proof might eventually be reversed or the merger notification might be considered incomplete. However, if there are legal provisions in the home country prohibiting the furnishing of information or presentation of documents to foreign competition policy authorities, the principles of international law require that the information sought be obtained by means of bilateral negotiations.

177. A request for information may be enforced without too much difficulty only when bilateral or multilateral mutual assistance agreements exist. However, similar agreements covering administrative proceedings do not yet exist. To close this gap – particularly as far as service is concerned – Section 57(1) sentence 3 of the Act against Restraints of Competition, concerning proceedings pursuant to Sections 22 to 24a of the Act, allows the decision requesting information to be served on the manager of the

domestic subsidiary, if he is considered authorised to accept service within the meaning of Section 8 of the Administrative Service Act, because the enterprise operates on the German market through its domestic subsidiary. In the absence of a person authorised to accept service, however, publication in the Federal Gazette will be considered service according to Section 57(1) sentence 4. If the enterprises fail to comply with the request, an administrative fine decision may in principle be issued against them, execution of which can be levied upon the subsidiary's property due to the economic unity existing among the affiliated enterprises.

3. Issues in extraterritorial remedies

178.   The problems discussed above in connection with obtaining information and service of process also apply to the enforcement of antitrust decisions concerning multinational enterprises.   On the other hand, this should not be interpreted as meaning that difficulties have always arisen.   For example, in the Zoja/CSC case, the Commission of the European Communities had no difficulty in imposing and recovering the fine levied on the U.S. firm, Commercial Solvents Corporation, for abuse of a dominant position within the Common Market. In the United States and in the European Communities, the parent or subsidiary established on national or community territory may be held accountable for restrictive practices exercised by branches of the multinational enterprise located abroad if they have participated in some way in the restrictive behaviour (see paragraphs 132 and 137 to 139 above). As in the case of requests for information, in some Member countries fewer difficulties appear to arise in enforcing decisions when the parent company is situated on national territory than when only a subsdiary is located there.

179.   Where the two conditions of national parent or subsidiary and its participation in the restriction do not exist problems of enforcement have arisen in most Member countries. A case in Denmark involving five leading linoleum manufacturers illustrates this point. The five manufacturers refused to supply a Danish purchasing organisation. The organisation then obtained supplies from a Danish wholesaler with the result that the said manufacturers discontinued supplies to the wholesaler with respect to goods which were to be resold to the purchasing organisation. The Monopolies Control Authority (M.C.A.) ordered the Danish agencies for the foreign manufacturers either to resume deliveries to the wholesaler or to accept the purchasing organisation as a customer on the same terms as those practised for other wholesalers. The agencies then submitted orders to the foreign factories from the two complainants but were told by the factories that the orders could not be fulfilled. As the restrictive practices of the foreign factories thus could not be brought to an end under the provisions of the Monopolies Control Act, the M.C.A. reported the case to the Minister of Commerce under Section 14 of the Monopolies Control Act.

180.   It appears that only the United States have in some cases succeeded in obtaining compliance with decisions involving multinational enterprises even when there is no branch of the firm located within its territorial jurisdiction. In this connection a distinction should however be made between decisions imposing a fine on foreign enterprises and those aiming at changing the behaviour or structure of the foreign enterprises. In the first case the fact that the United States and the European Communities constitute important markets which multinational enterprises are obliged to enter sooner or later must be an incentive for them to comply with decisions imposing fines for anticompetitive behaviour[189]. The situation in the European Communities is similar in that no particular difficulty has so far arisen as regards enforcement of decisions on account of the multinationality of a group of enterprises, the centre of decision of which lies outside the Community. All these decisions have been enforced, whether

or not they have been challenged before the Court of Justice. In the "Dyestuffs" case, the Ciba Company, which did not appeal against the decision concerning it, paid the fine after publication in the Official Journal of the European Communities of the Geigy and Sandoz judgments.

181.   Decisions designed to change the behaviour or the structure of foreign enterprises seem to raise greater enforcement difficulties and they may give rise to real conflicts of sovereignty between States in cases where it is a foreign law which has required the enterprises to engage in the restrictive activities complained of.   There are two limited defences which may be invoked by enterprises whose extraterritorial conduct would otherwise be subject to prosecution under United States antitrust laws. The first defence is that such conduct is compelled by a foreign sovereign. The second is that such conduct is interrelated with the public acts of a foreign sovereign within its territory. The scope of both defences has not been precisely determined under decided United States cases. As to the first defence, that of foreign governmental compulsion: on the one hand, in Interamerican Refining Corp. v. Texaco Maracaibo, Inc.[190] defendants, subsidiaries of American parents, were charged with refusing to sell oil to an American plaintiff. They successfully justified their action on the ground that the Venezuelan Government had decreed that no oil could leave Venezuela intended for sale or resale to the plaintiff. On the other hand, in Sabre Shipping Company v. American President Lines, Ltd.[191], another District Court stated, as dictum, that Japanese shippers are not necessarily immunised from U.S. antitrust enforcement, as to acts in U.S. commerce and outside Japan, on the ground that such acts were directed by the Japanese Government. A court's response to the assertion of such a defence is likely to turn, as with the enforcement of subpoenas against foreign nationals notwithstanding contrary foreign law, on the principles of comity set forth in paragraph 142, supra. The second defence, that of act of state, is the contention that when the real or primary cause of the injury to competition was a sovereign act of a foreign state within its territory, U.S. antitrust law is not applicable. In American Banana Co. v. United Fruit Co.[192], the United Fruit Company allegedly induced Costa Rica to send troops into territory now a part of Panama. This military action added land to Costa Rica and drove out the plaintiff, the only significant competitor in the production of bananas for distribution to the United States. The Supreme Court dismissed the suit, citing the act of state doctrine. A more recent case which appears to follow this precedent is Occidental Petroleum Corporation v. Buttes Gas & Oil Company[193]. Eighteen years after American Banana, in United States v. Sisal Sales Corporation[194], U.S. defendants solicited and obtained passage of Mexican federal and state legislation facilitating establishment of a cartel of sisal producers which operated through an exclusive sales corporation in the United States. The Supreme Court found a violation of the antitrust laws in that the defendants by their acts in the United States and elsewhere had brought about forbidden results in the United States -- with foreign governmental participation being viewed as merely incidental. While uncertainty remains as to the scope of these two defences, it is clear that mere authorisation of defendants' conduct under foreign law, as opposed to conduct compelled of defendant under foreign law, is generally not a defence to the application of United States antitrust laws.[195]

4.   Issues in dealing with intra-corporate transactions

182. As regards those practices referred to as "individual" i.e. those which are operated by a single multinational enterprise, issues have arisen when an attempt has been made to apply national laws to actions resulting from a directive or instruction from a parent company to its subsidiary due to the fact that the laws do not usually apply to such directives or instructions when they merely consist in a division of tasks within one and the same economic entity[196].   There are obvious difficulties in at-

tempting to require that enterprises which are distinct from the legal point of view but which form a single economic unit with a central organisation, should compete among themselves. However, the rules of competition of a Member country or of the European Communities are applicable when individual restrictive business practices take the form of abuse of a dominant position or of monopolistic behaviour in the national market, or where they constitute an individual restrictive business practice such as, for example, a refusal to sell or an illegal form of discrimination.

183. Thus, the provisions relating to competition contained in the Treaty of Rome setting up the European Communities are applicable to internal directives, agreements or practices between parent companies and subsidiaries to the extent that they constitute restrictions of competition affecting third parties as, for example, in the Kodak case[197] where identical conditions of sale were applied by subsidiaries on the instruction of the parent company and were therefore considered by the Commission as "agreements" between enterprises, since they necessarily form the object of a contract between the Kodak companies and their resellers. They will also be applicable to contracts of the same kind designed to isolate national markets or maintain price disparities between Member states, or whose object or effect is to restrict the freedom of competition of other firms. On the other hand, the Court of Justice of the European Communities declared in the Centrafarm case[198] that Article 85 of the Treaty of Rome was not concerned with "agreements or concerted practices between undertakings belonging to the same concern and having the status of parent company and subsidiary, if the undertakings form an economic unit within which the subsidiary has no real freedom to determine its course of action on the market, and if the agreements or practices are concerned merely with the internal allocation of tasks as between the undertakings".

184. In the United States, agreements or decisions between a parent company and its subsidiaries are not treated as illegal if trade outside the affiliated companies is not affected by the restrictions. The degree of control exercised by the parent company over its subsidiaries, or by the subsidiaries over the parent company, and the degree to which the affiliated companies keep themselves separate as competitors, are all factors which the Courts have to take into consideration in order to decide whether the behaviour of such companies justifies an examination under Section 1 of the Sherman Act. Thus, in the case of the United States v. Timken Roller Bearing Co.[199] the Supreme Court accepted that there had been intra-enterprise conspiracy in the foreign commerce area. That case involved an agreement between an American firm producing between 70 and 80 per cent of American tapered roller bearings and two former British and French rivals which had become partially owned by, and affiliated with, American Timken. The agreement involved the allocation of trade territories, fixed prices on products which might be sold in markets of the others, and restricted imports to and exports from the United States. In holding the agreements illegal the Court treated them as being between persons and companies who were "legally separate" from each other. In these conditions the agreements were not accepted as merely an arrangement within a single corporate entity, but were deemed to be an arrangement between competitors using a joint operation as a device to effectuate illegal objectives.

5. *Problems resulting from divergencies in the laws of Member countries*

185. The previous sections of this chapter have described a number of obstacles to the extraterritorial application of national legislation to the restrictive business practices of multinational enterprises. These are however not the only kinds of problems involved in dealing with these practices. There are wider and more complex issues. Fundamental differences exist between Member countries in the substantive legal provisions they

have adopted to control restrictive business practices, which make international co-operative action, to the extent necessary to cope with restrictive business practices emanating from abroad, that much more difficult to achieve. These differences may be seen in the basic approaches of national legislation to the general problem of control of restraints of competition, in the actual scope of legislation, in the procedural methods used in applying it and in the remedies available to combat infringements.

186. At the level of basic principles enshrined in national competition laws, considerable variations are evident according to whether the pursuit of competition is considered the sole aim or whether it is considered one of many elements in evaluating behaviour of enterprises. These divergencies are reflected especially in the attitudes towards the control of mergers and abuses by dominant enterprises. Only six Member countries – Australia, Canada, Germany, Japan, the United Kingdom and the United States – and the European Coal and Steel Community have introduced special control of mergers while the remainder have no form of preventive control. In a number of other Member countries the legislation on restrictive business practices contains some provisions applicable to mergers, for example registration of certain operations in order to collect more information on mergers, but these provisions do not constitute a comprehensive system of merger control. The countries involved here are Austria, Belgium, Spain, Sweden and the EEC.

187. In addition, several countries prohibit outright a number of restrictive business practices such as resale price maintenance, refusal to sell, collusive tendering and price discrimination while several others treat all or most on a case-by-case basis with no presumptions for or against particular practices. In the field of industrial property rights certain clauses in patent licensing agreements are considered anti-competitive in some countries but are accepted as necessary to the exercise of patent rights in others. In the control of monopolies or dominant enterprises, among which multinational enterprises are frequently to be found, there are especially marked differences. Countries which control abusive behaviour of market dominating enterprises are led to examine most economic data such as costs, prices and profits and require therefore detailed information on these factors from the enterprises under investigation. This information may be needed to ensure a proper assessment of the behaviour of a multinational enterprise and may not be forthcoming solely from the nationally based parent or subsidiary.

188. Important divergencies exist also in regard to the procedure followed in pursuing restrictive business practices as well as the sanctions prescribed. Legislation on restrictive business practices is sometimes based on criminal proceedings, providing for the hearing of witnesses, subpoenas to ensure the appearance of certain persons or the production of certain information. All such proceedings may be frustrated if proof or witnesses have to be sought outside national jurisdiction.

189. Two main conclusions may be drawn from the existence of these divergencies between Member countries. In the first place, the affiliates of a multinational group established in several different countries are therefore subject to a wide variation of laws on restrictive business practices which they may be able to exploit to conclude restrictive agreements or engage in or disguise restrictive behaviour tolerated in one country but disfavoured in another. The second point is that it would be unrealistic to expect full international co-operation in the form of an international convention in the absence of greater similarity in national laws.

Chapter Three

POSSIBLE REMEDIES AND SUGGESTIONS FOR ACTION

I. Introduction

190. The material collected for the purpose of this report identifies a number of an-titrust and competition policy problems connected with multinational enterprises without, however, providing a sufficient factual basis for quantifying their relative importance. The fact that this report essentially concentrates on problems does not imply a negative judgment about the overall competitive effects of multinational enterprises. Chapter I of this report shows that such enterprises can also produce substantial beneficial effects on national and international competition. This is particulary true in cases of concentrated national markets, especially if they are characterised by high bar-riers to entry or do not enjoy the pro-competitive effects of international trade because of tariff or non-tariff barriers. It should also be emphasized that multinational enterprises are not a homogeneous group and that the policy aim to maximise their beneficial and minimise their detrimental effects on competition has to take due ac-count of the fact that they range from the fairly small firm with a single overseas sub-sidiary to the big concern with major enterprises in many countries.

191. Multinational enterprises may raise specific antitrust and competition policy problems because of a number of factors. First, multinational enterprises are often superior to national enterprises in absolute size and in terms of the sophistication of their technological and managerial performance. Second, multinationals are more often found to be operating in oligopolistic markets than are national enterprises. As a consequence of these factors, multinational enterprises frequently wield more economic power than most of the national enterprises with which they compete and they therefore play a special role in national and international concentration. This means, in effect, that when a multinational enterprise does engage in restrictive business practices the economic significance and geographic reach of these practices tends to be greater than that of similar practices engaged in by a national enterprise. This is true, according to the material collected for the purpose of this report, of mergers, as well as of the alloca-tion of production and markets, pricing practices and practices in connection with in-dustrial property rights.

192. In addition, by their very nature large multinational enterprises frequently operate in separate national markets by means of legally distinct entities, some only partially owned. They, like national firms operating through separate entities, engage in ar-rangements with their subsidiaries or affiliates, which would violate competition laws or rules if engaged in between wholly independent firms. Thus, an issue arises whether or to what extent it is possible or desirable to have competition rules and remedies app-ly to such intra-enterprise practices.

193. It should be emphasized that large national enterprises may present many problems similar to be those just discussed. Restrictive practices of multinational enterprises do not differ in terms of competition theory or in terms of the substantive antitrust rules of Member countries. It does not therefore seem necessary or appropriate to seek to create different substantive antitrust laws for national and multinational enterprises. Such different substantive antitrust rules could have the effect of handicapping some competitors as against others.

194. In applying national antitrust procedures certain difficulties in controlling the restrictive business practices of multinational enterprises come to light. The material collected for this report shows that the national antitrust authorities encounter problems relating to the service of documents, the enforcement of decisions and in particular the collection of information more frequently in cases involving multinational enterprises than in those concerning only national firms. Once again, these problems are not exclusive to multinational enterprises. They can and do also arise in connection with international cartels and in cases involving enterprises having significant export or import activities.

II. Possible remedies

195. The following possible remedies are discussed from two points of view : whether they are capable of solving or mitigating the problems identified in this report and whether they are useful and likely to be accepted by Member countries in the not too distant future. No attempt is made to suggest one measure to solve all problems, but rather a set of possible remedies is proposed which, taken together, may lead in this direction. A wide range of proposals is included, envisaging, among other things, the creation of new procedures to obtain more information about multinational enterprises at national and international levels, the development of international consultation, conciliation and arbitration procedures, or of voluntary codes of good conduct, standards of behaviour or guidelines for enterprises and governments, and even the creation of a binding international antitrust law and an international agency with powers of enforcement. In discussing such possible remedies, a distinction is made between possible action by the business community itself and possible remedies at national and at international levels.

1. *By the business community*

196. Action by the business community itself would be a first step, and would be of a voluntary nature. It would consist of avoiding conduct clearly at variance with competition guidelines[200], particularly in situations where affected countries may not apply their laws and policies effectively due to the international character of the enterprise or practices in question. Co-operation in furnishing information beyond legal obligations seems already to be taking place in some Member countries. It should be further encouraged, in particular with regard to relevant information located outside the national territory and in the possession of corporate entities other than the one doing business on national territory. To a certain extent, voluntary co-operation seems also to be possible in relation to the service of documents. Enterprises could occasionally waive any rights they might have as to methods or place of service in the interests of a speedy procedure and resolution of legal issues.

2. At the national level

197. Probably the most effective measures to solve or mitigate the problems identified in this report would consist of national legislative action. At the present time, there are no institutions in the world with powers comparable to those of governments. The experience of countries with more sophisticated competition laws and policies shows that the introduction or strengthening of antitrust laws and competition policies could substantially contribute to solving not only a significant number of the problems connected with the activities of multinational enterprises but also those of national enterprises. As only governments have the power to take such legislative measures, they also have the responsibility for considering such action in the first instance.

198. Legislative action could solve a substantial number of the problems of national and international economic concentration in relevant markets in which multinational enterprises play a significant role. This could be done by introducing or strengthening, if one already exists, a system of merger control utilising an analysis of the competitive effects of mergers, whether involving multinational or domestic enterprises, with, if deemed necessary, appropriate powers of divestiture or dissolution according to the needs of the countries concerned.

199. Legislative action by Member countries could also include the introduction or, if one already exists, the strengthening of a system of abuse control over economically powerful or market dominating enterprises, among which most multinational enterprises are to be found. Experience in those Member countries which already have a workable system of abuse control shows that many substantive problems relating to powerful enterprises, not necessarily excluding those which may be created by arrangements among affiliated enterprises, can be alleviated under such a system.

200. It does not appear that restrictive agreement legislation is directed at purely intra-corporate conduct for the reasons discussed below. Competition laws and policies in the OECD Member nations generally provide that intra-enterprise practices such as allocation of functions among branches or subsidiaries of a single enterprise are not considered in themselves as an unreasonable restraint of trade. Holding such practices unlawful would be likely to discourage internal growth and decrease efficiency. It might also force upon competition authorities the impracticable task of seeking to create and maintain competition within a single enterprise on an ongoing basis. In no case have arrangements within the same legal entity, such as between branches or operating divisions of the same company, been held to be unlawful. Even in cases involving separate legal entities under common control, findings of illegality have been rare and have been based upon exhaustive factual analysis of the particular cases. In certain instances of arrangements between legally separate entities with partial common ownership which eliminated significant pre-existing or potential competition among the entities or which injured competition outside the enterprise by means for instance, of agreed refusals to deal, illegality has been found.

201. A third field in which legislative action by governments could help to resolve problems is that of industrial, commercial and intellectual property rights. Legislation or regulatory action might follow the lines suggested in the OECD Recommendation concerning action against restrictive business practices relating to the use of patents and licences of 22nd January, 1974 referred to in paragraph 100 above (see Annex III).

202. Governmental action introducing or strengthening merger control systems, control over abuses by economically powerful enterprises and competition rules prohibiting the abuse of industrial, commercial and intellectual property rights are not the only measures capable of diminishing the problems identified in this report although they would certainly be among those which might be expected to have the

most far-reaching results. Taking into account the great diversity of laws and policies existing in Member countries it seems to be impossible to draw up a complete list of possibilities for legislative action. In those Member countries, however, which do not yet have legislation prohibiting horizontal and vertical restrictive agreements or a workable abuse control system regulating them, serious consideration might be given to introducing such legislation. A number of Member countries have found it effective to apply their legislation to restrictive conduct which has a substantial, direct and foreseeable effect on the country applying its law.

203. A further possibility for action by governments relates more specifically to antitrust procedure. One of the central problems identified in this report is that of collecting relevant information controlled by a multinational enterprise which is located outside the national territory, for purposes of an investigation of conduct affecting the jurisdiction. One of the elements contributing to this problem is the very nature of the multinational enterprise with units in various countries. Additional problems may be created by the reluctance of enterprises to co-operate in providing such information. It therefore seems appropriate that countries should consider, in conformity with the established rules of international law and taking into account international comity, the development of national procedures with a view to enhancing their ability to obtain relevant information which is outside of their territory but which is within the control of the multinational enterprise concerned and which is necessary to the enforcement of national antitrust laws and the disclosure of which is not contrary to the law of the place where the information is located. For example, in certain circumstances, it might be appropriate to interpret non-compliance to the disadvantage of the enterprise which cannot justify such non-compliance. An appropriate legal test for demanding such information may be whether the parent or subsidiary outside the jurisdiction and its affiliate in the jurisdiction both participated actively in the transaction being investigated, or whether the foreign parent actively supervised a local affiliate which did participate.

204. Another problem is the existence in some states of legislation or policies which preclude an enterprise from providing business-related information to foreign governments. A possibility for action by governments to solve this problem would be, perhaps in the context of bilateral or multilateral understandings, appropriate modification of national laws preventing disclosure of relevant information by or concerning multinational enterprises so as to allow disclosure to competition authorities of other jurisdictions under proper procedures and safeguards. However, where these laws are of general application, such modification may raise problems which go beyond issues of competition policy.

3. At international level

205. At the international level, action may mainly be taken by governments and by international organisations. As to the action of governments at the international level, the least complicated possibility seems to be that of bilateral arrangements, agreements or formal treaties. They could cover a wide variety of subjects, ranging from the exchange of generally available information to the creation of a common antitrust law. As to the first possibility, it should be noted that OECD Member countries already have the opportunity to utilise or develop other procedures dealing with the exchange of information at the OECD level (cf. paragraph 206 below). However, Member countries might more readily exchange information which is not generally available on a bilateral basis with countries with similar antitrust and competition philosophies. Bilateral agreements relating to the exchange of information, consultation, conciliation or mutual administrative and judicial aid might well be useful and could lead to further developments which would help to overcome the problems identified in this report. Ef-

fectively functioning co-operation may lead the participating countries towards further harmonization of their antitrust laws and competition policies or co-ordination of investigations or procedures, a development which is also desirable from the viewpoint of enterprises doing business in these countries, since it would provide more certainty than currently exists. Also, third countries might, if co-operation was effective between the parties to a bilateral treaty, either wish to join the arrangement in order to mitigate their own problems in the field of antitrust and competition policy, or decide to conclude similar agreements with other countries closer to them in terms of their laws and policies.

206. On a more than bilateral and less than global level, a number of international organisations can and do help to reduce the problems identified in this report. The OECD Recommendation of 5th October, 1967 concerning co-operation between Member countries on restrictive business practices affecting international trade (see Annex I) and the OECD Recommendation of 3rd July, 1973 concerning a consultation and conciliation procedure on restrictive business practices affecting international trade (see Annex II) are procedures which, without discriminating between national and multinational enterprises, may help to iron out some of the problems in question here. The 1967 Recommendation established a voluntary procedure for prior notification of antitrust investigations and proceedings by Member countries when important interests of another Member country are involved. It also provided for the co-ordination of antitrust enforcement, co-operation in developing or applying mutually beneficial methods of dealing with restrictive business practices in international trade and exchanges of information on antitrust matters to the extent possible. Most of the notifications and requests for information which have been made since 1968 related to multinational enterprises. Certain of these notifications have approached being a form of voluntary consultation procedure aimed at achieving mutually agreed adjustments through discussions among the Member countries concerned. Such a development is in line with the 1973 Council Recommendation, although this Recommendation has never been specifically invoked in practice. Member countries may consider making specific use of this Recommendation, altering it or suggesting alternative proposals.

207. At the regional level, the European Communities have adopted a highly sophisticated antitrust law which, once a system of merger control is introduced, will be among the most comprehensive legislations in the world. It is no more difficult for the Commission, which is the regional antitrust authority having its own powers of enforcement, to enforce its legislation than it is for a national authority to enforce national law ; it may take action directly within the territory of all Member States and not only in one of them. Although in the European Communities national laws relating to competition may apply simultaneously, implying that there may be parallel procedures, the fact that there is a fairly comprehensive legislation and an effective competition policy in the European Communities has allowed substantial results to be achieved in regard to the restrictive practices of multinational enterprises the scope of which extends beyond purely national territory.

208. At the OECD level, a common antitrust law comparable to that of the European Communities is not realistically achievable. There are, however, a number of ways other than the OECD Recommendations of 1967 and 1973 in which OECD could help to reduce some of the problems identified above. The Committee believes that the OECD voluntary guidelines contained in the Declaration on International Investment and Multinational Enterprises adopted by the OECD Council, meeting at Ministerial level, on 21st June, 1976, relating to competition and the shaping of corporate conduct in a general way (see Annex IV), should serve useful purposes. Of course, to some extent guidelines dealing with difficult legal and economic concepts such as abuse of a dominant position and adverse effects on competition cannot in themselves provide

precise rules for business executives to follow in specific circumstances. Under the national law of various countries, these concepts have been given meaning only through interpretation by the competent tribunals. However, the Committee considered that such guidelines could nonetheless provide useful standards for enterprises and could be of value in helping to achieve a common approach towards multinational enterprises as well as acceptable relationships between multinational enterprises and countries whose trade they affect. In addition, they could contribute to the further development of widely accepted standards within OECD and at world level.

209. Even though certain courses of action may be suggested to Member governments this does not mean that the OECD should cease to study multinational enterprises from various antitrust and competition policy viewpoints. Although the development of an international antitrust law and the creation of an international antitrust authority can only be a long-run posssibility, this issue is still being discussed at international level. As most parent companies of multinational enterprises are located in OECD Member countries, among which are to be found those with the most developed antitrust laws, it seems appropriate for the OECD to keep in touch through its Committee of Experts on Restrictive Business Practices with endeavours to establish international antitrust principles and institutions. In addition, it seems appropriate for the OECD to study, through the same Committee, other means of coping with the problems identified in the report in connection with its other work and, at the same time, to endeavour to identify the problems still more precisely in order to achieve a better understanding of their importance and a better basis for the consideration of possible remedies.

III. Suggestions for action

210. In accordance with the considerations set forth in paragraph 198, it is suggested that Member countries which have not yet done so consider the introduction of a workable system of merger control or the strengthening of an already introduced but not effectively functioning merger control system. As regards the criteria to be observed, it is sufficient to refer to the Committee's report on mergers, published by OECD in 1975, paragraphs 185 and 186 of which read as follows :

"185. The accelerating trend towards merger together with the already high level of concentration in a number of economic sectors draws attention to the problems of competition which are created by changing market structures and it seems therefore appropriate at the present time to suggest to Member countries which have not yet done so to consider the adoption of an effective system of merger control.

186. The following characteristics might be taken into account :
   i) a procedure for registering mergers, wherever this is felt necessary ;
   ii) a system to facilitate obtaining information about occurrenceof major mergers, such as requiring their prior notification ;
   iii) minimum quantitative criteria below which mergers would not be subject to control ;
   iv) objective criteria or presumpions for use in evaluating mergers ;
   v) reasonable time limits for deciding initially whether to allow or challenge certain mergers."

211. In accordance with paragraph 199 above, it is suggested that Member countries which have not yet done so consider the creation of a workable abuse control procedure, the strengthening of an already existing abuse control procedure for market domi-

nating and economically powerful enterprises or the creation or strengthening of legislation against monopolisation or attempts to monopolise.

212. With reference to the matters considered in paragraph 200 above, the Committee has no changes to recommend at this time in relation to the treatment of intra-corporate arrangements.

213. In accordance with paragraph 201 above, it is suggested that Member countries consider legislation or regulatory action against restrictive business practices relating to the use of patents and licences.

214. In accordance with paragraph 203 above, it is suggested that Member countries consider how they could develop appropriate procedures to facilitate investigation and discovery by their antitrust authorities in regard to information located outside their national territory, in conformity with the rules of public international law and taking into account international comity.

215. Also, in accordance with paragraphs 203 and 204 above, it is suggested that Member countries might, where discretion exists, consider whether and, if so, how and under what safeguards to provide or allow disclosure of information relevant to the enforcement of national antitrust laws and to national competition policy purposes but which at present may not be obtainable or transmissible to other Member countries for legal reasons.

216. In accordance with paragraph 205 above, it is suggested that Member countries consider the possibility of concluding bilateral or multilateral treaties on mutual administrative and judicial aid with other Member countries which would be applicable to the enforcement of restrictive business practices laws.

217. In view of the advisability of taking action in regard to the problems identified in this report not only at national and bilateral levels, it is suggested that Member countries make use as far as possible of the OECD Recommendation of 1967 concerning co-operation between Member countries on restrictive business practices affecting international trade and continue to explore possible use of the Recommendation of 1973 concerning a consultation and conciliation procedure on restrictive business practices affecting international trade.

218. The OECD Committee of Experts on Restrictive Business Practices will keep under review antitrust and competition policy problems identified in this report and try, as part of its future programme of work, to study these problems in greater depth in order to develop more adequate measures to remedy them. The Committee will in particular keep in touch with all endeavours at the international level to deal with antitrust and competition policy problems connected with multinational enterprises.

Annex I

RECOMMENDATION OF THE COUNCIL
CONCERNING CO-OPERATION BETWEEN MEMBER COUNTRIES
ON RESTRICTIVE BUSINESS PRACTICES
AFFECTING INTERNATIONAL TRADE

(Adopted by the Council on 5th October, 1967)[201]

The Council,

Having regard to Article 5(b) of the Convention on the Organisation for Economic Co-operation and Development of 14th December, 1960 ;

Having regard to the Resolution of the Council of 5th December, 1961, concerning Action in the Field of Restrictive Business Practices and the Establishment of a Committee of Experts ;

Having regard to the Report by the Committee of Experts on Restrictive Business Practices concerning Co-operation Between Member Countries on Restrictive Business Practices Affecting International Trade ;

Recognising that the diminution of free competition through restrictive business practices may have an adverse effect on achievement of the trade-expansion and economic-growth aims of Member countries as set out in Article 1 of the Convention ;

Recognising that closer co-operation between Member countries is needed in this field but that the present powers of the authorities of Member countries to co-operate are limited to various degrees ;

Recognising, moreover, that the unilateral application of national legislation, in cases where business operations in other countries are involved, raises questions as to the respective spheres of sovereignty of the countries concerned ;

Considering therefore that a closer co-operation between Member countries in the form of consultations, exchanges of information and co-ordination of efforts on a fully voluntary basis should be encouraged it being understood that such co-operation should not in any way be construed to affect the legal positions of Member countries with regard to such questions of sovereignty, and in particular the extra-territorial application of laws concerning restrictive business practices, as may arise ;

I. **Recommends** to the Governments of Member countries.

1. (a) That in so far as their laws permit, when Member countries undertake under their restrictive business practices laws an investigation or a proceeding involving important interests of another Member country, they should notify such Member country in a manner and at a time deemed appropriate. Notification should, where appropriate, take place in advance in order to enable the proceeding Member country, while retaining full freedom of ultimate decision, to take account of such views as the other Member country may wish to express and of such remedial action as the other Member country may find it feasible to take under its own laws to deal with the restrictive business practice.

(b) That where two or more Member countries proceed against a restrictive business practice in international trade, they should endeavour to co-ordinate their action in so far as appropriate and practicable under national laws.

2. To supply each other with any information on restrictive business practices in international trade which their laws and legitimate interests permit them to disclose.

3. To co-operate in developing or applying mutually beneficial methods of dealing with restrictive business practices in international trade.

II. **Instructs** the Committee of Experts on Restrictive Business Practices to keep under review developments connected with the present Recommendation and to examine periodically the progress made in thi field.

Annex II

RECOMMENDATION OF THE COUNCIL
CONCERNING A CONSULTATION AND CONCILIATION
PROCEDURE ON RESTRICTIVE BUSINESS PRACTICES
AFFECTING INTERNATIONAL TRADE

(Adopted by the Council on 3rd July, 1973)

The Council,

Having regard to Article 5(*b*) of the Convention on the Organisation for Economic Co-operation anc Development of 14th December, 1960 ;

Having regard to the Resolution of the Council of 5th December, 1961, concerning Action in the Field of Restrictive Business Practices and the Establishment of a Committee of Experts ;

Having regard to the Recommendation of the Council of 5th October, 1967, concerning Co-operatior between Member Countries on Restrictive Business Practices Affecting International Trade ;

Having regard to the Report by the Committee of Experts on Restrictive Business Practices of 4th June 1973, concerning a Consultation and Conciliation Procedure on Restrictive Business Practices Affecting International Trade ;

Recognising that restrictive business practices may constitute an obstacle to the achievement of the economic growth and trade expansion aims of Member countries and may contribute to the inflationary process ;

Recognising that closer co-operation between Member countries is needed to deal effectively with restrictive business practices operated by enterprises situated in Member countries when they affect the interests of one or more other Member countries and when they have a harmful effect on international trade ;

Considering that a consultation and conciliation procedure in this field should be provided on a voluntary basis, it being understood that such co-operation should not in any way be construed to affect the legal positions of Member countries, in particular with regard to such questions of sovereignty and extraterritorial application of laws concerning restrictive business practices, as may arise ;

I. **Recommends** to the Governments of Member countries :

1. That a Member country which considers that one or more enterprises situated in one or more other Member countries are engaging in restrictive business practices which substantially and adversely affect its interests, should request consultation with such other Member country or countries ;

2. That any Member country so addressed should give full consideration to the case submitted by the requesting country and, in particular, to the nature of the restrictive business practices in question, the enterprises engaging in them and the alleged harmful effects on the interests of the requesting country and on international trade ;

3. That the Member country addressed which agrees that enterprises situated in its territory engage in restrictive business practices harmful to the interests of the requesting country should attempt to ensure that these enterprises take remedial action, or should itself take whatever remedial action it considers appropriate, in particular under its legislation on restrictive business practices, on a voluntary basis and considering its legitimate interests ;

4. That, in the event of a satisfactory settlement of the case, the requesting country, in agreement with, and in the form accepted by, the Member country or countries addressed, should inform the Committee of Experts on Restrictive Business Practices of the nature of the restrictive business practices in question and of the remedial measures taken by the Member country or countries addressed ;

5.   That, in the event that no satisfactory solution can be found, because the country or one of the countries addressed does not agree that enterprises situated in its territory engage in the alleged practices, or that such practices are restrictive or that they have harmful effects, or because it feels unable to take any action under its laws or for whatever other reason, the Member countries concerned, if they so agree, should submit the case to the Committee of Experts on Restrictive Business Practices with a view to conciliation. If the Member countries concerned agree to the use of another means of settlement, and do not therefore submit the case to the Committee, they should, if they consider it appropriate, inform the Committee of such features of the settlement as they feel they can disclose.

II.   **Instructs** the Committee of Experts on Restrictive Business Practices :

1.   To consider the reports submitted by Member countries in accordance with paragraph 4 of Section I above :

2.   To consider the requests for conciliation submitted by Member countries in accordance with paragraph 5 of Section I above and to assist, by offering advice or by any other means, in the settlement of the case between the Member countries concerned ;

3.   To report to the Council before 31st December, 1975 on the application of the present Recommendation and to submit proposals, where appropriate, for improving its implementation.

Annex III

RECOMMENDATION OF THE COUNCIL CONCERNING ACTION AGAINST RESTRICTIVE BUSINESS PRACTICES RELATING TO THE USE OF PATENTS AND LICENCES[202] (Adopted by the Council on 22nd January, 1974)

The Council,

Having regard to Article 5(*b*) of the Convention on the Organisation for Economic Co-operation and Development of 14th December, 1960 ;

Having regard to the Resolution of the Council of 5th December, 1961, concerning Action in the Field of Restrictive Business Practices and the Establishment of a Committee of Experts ;

Having regard to the Recommendation of the Council of 5th October, 1967, concerning Co-operation between Member countries on Restrictive Business Practices Affecting International Trade ;

Having regard to the Recommendation of the Council of 14th and 15th December, 1971, concerning Action against Inflatiol in the Field of Competition Policy and, in particular, Section I, paragraph 1, sub-paragraph (*i*) (*c*) thereof ;

Having regard to the Recommendation of the Council of 3rd July, 1973, concerning a Consultation and Conciliation Procedure on Restrictive Business Practices Affecting International Trade ;

Having regard to the Report by the Committee of Experts on Restrictive Business Practices of 11th September, 1972, on Restrictive Business Practices relating to Patents and Licences and, in particular, paragraph 49 thereof :

Recognising that it is desirable to scrutinise and remedy the harmful effects of abusive restrictive business practices relating to the use of patents and licences since economic development is dependent on the dissemination of scientific and technological innovation through patents and that by granting licences subject to unjustifiable restrictions firms can use the rights attaching to the patents to exercise excessive economic power :

I.   **Recommends** to the Governments of Member countries:

1.   That they should be particularly alert to harmful effects on national and international trade which may result from abusive practices in which patentees and their licensees may engage, and, in particular, from the following :

(*a*) when negotiating or operating patent pools or cross-licensing agreements, unjustifiably imposing territorial, quantity or price restrictions or attempting to dominate an industry, market or new industrial process ;

(*b*) by means of territorial restrictions in patent licences affecting international trade, unjustifiably prohibiting exports of patented products or unjustifiably restricting trade in or exports of the patented products to specified areas ;

(*c*) by means of clauses concerning tied sales, obliging the licensee to obtain goods from the licensor or his designated sources, when the tied sales are not justified, for instance, by technical reasons concerning the quality of the goods manufactured under the licence ;

(*d*) by means of grant-back clauses, unjustifiably requiring the licensee to assign or grant back to the licensor exclusively all improvements discovered in working the patents when the effect of this practice is to reinforce the dominant position of the licensor or to stifle the licensee's incentive to invent ;

(*e*) by means of clauses unjustifiably limiting competition, preventing one or more parties to the patent licensing contract from competing with other parties to the contract, or with third persons in other industrial fields not covered by the licensed patent ;

(*f*) arbitrarily grouping and licensing all patents in a particular field and refusing to grant licences for only some of the patents or using other forms of package licensing when these practices are coercive in character and when the selection of the patents is not negotiated for the convenience of the parties ;

(*g*) contrary to national law, fixing the prices of patented products by means of patent licences.

2.   That they should give consideration to the desirability and feasibility of compulsory licensing of patents and, where possible, related know-how as a remedy to restore competition where such patents have been misused contrary to their restrictive business practices laws, when such a remedy is not already provided for in their legislation.

3.   That they should give consideration to the desirability and feasibility of making available to the competent authorities procedures for the registration of international licensing agreements, when such procedures are not already provived for in their legislation.

II.   **Instructs** the Committee of Experts on Restrictive Business Practices to keep under review the application of the present Recommendation and to report to the Council when appropriate.

Annex IV

EXTRACT FROM THE OECD GUIDELINES FOR MULTINATIONAL ENTERPRISES RELATING TO COMPETITION

Competition

Enterprises should

While conforming to official competition rules and established policies of the countries in which they operate,

1.   Refrain from actions which would adversely affect competition in the relevant market by abusing a dominant position of market power, by means of, for example,

(*a*) anti-competitive acquisitions,

(*b*) predatory behaviour toward competitors,

(*c*) unreasonable refusal to deal,

(*d*) anti-competitive abuse of industrial property rights,

(e) discriminatory (i.e. unreasonable differentiated) pricing and using such pricing transactions between affiliated enterprises as a means of affecting adversely competition outside these enterprises ;

2.   Allow purchasers, distributors and licensees freedom to resell, export, purchase and develop their operations consistent with law, trade conditions, the need for specialisation and sound commercial practice ;

3.   Refrain from participating in or otherwise purposely strengthening the restrictive effects of international or domestic cartels or restrictive agreements which adversely affect or eliminate competition and which are not generally or specifically accepted under applicable national or international legislation ;

4.   Be ready to consult and co-operate, including the provision of information, with competent authorities of countries whose interests are directly affected in regard to competition issues or investigations. Provision of information should be in accordance with safeguards normally applicable in this field.

NOTES AND REFERENCES

1. Figures quoted in the United Nations report "Multinational Corporations in World Development", United Nations Department of Economic and Social Affairs, New York, 1973, pp. 6-7 and 13.

2. Throughout the report the words "national" and "Member countries" should be understood as applying where appropriate also to the European Communities.

3. See in particular "Multinational Corporations in World Development", United Nations, Department of Economic and Social Affairs, New York, 1973, Annexe II.

4. See section III below : " Extent of the Phenomenon", para. 13 et seq.

5. Cf. C. Tugendhat, The Multinationals, London, 1971, p. 10.

6. According to Dunning's estimates, the share of portfolio investments in the foreign investments mentioned amounted to 90 per cent (cf. J.H. Dunning (ed.), The Multinational Enterprise, Guildford and London, 1971, p. 16).

7. Cf. here and in the following in particular R. Vernon, Antitrust and International Business, Harvard Business Review, September - October, 1968, pp. 78 et seq.

8. Cf. F.W. Fröhlich, Multinationale Unternehmen – Entstehung, Organisation und Management, Baden-Baden, 1974, p. 27 ; according to Tugendhat, United States direct investments in Europe amounted to $1.4 thousand million in 1926 and to $1 thousand million in 1946 (cf. C. Tugendhat, op. cit. p. 12).

9. Cf. F.W. Fröhlich, op. cit., p. 30 ; also Multinational Corporations in World Development, op. cit., p. 146.

10. Cf. Multinational Enterprises in World Development, op. cit., p. 146.

11. Cf. F.W. Fröhlich, op. cit., p. 26.

12. Cf. Multinational Enterprises in World Development, op. cit., p. 238 ; "minimum number of affiliates" refers to the number of "links" between parent corporations and host countries. Two or more affiliates of a particular corporation in a given foreign country are counted as one "link".

13. Cf. C. Tugendhat, op. cit., p. 17.

14. Cf. The Impact of Foreign Direct Investment on the United Kingdom, Department of Trade and Industry, by M.E. Steuer and others (Steuer Report), London, 1973, p. 195.

15. Cf. C. Tugendhat, op. cit., p. 16.

16. Cf. i. a. R. Vernon, Antitrust and International Business, op. cit., p. 83.

17. See Multinational Corporations in World Development, op. cit., p. 13.

18. Ibid., p. 13 et seq.

19. The average annual growth rate of the gross domestic product of market economies at current prices was 9 per cent in the period 1961 to 1971 compared with an average annual growth rate of international production estimated on the basis of sales at current prices of United States foreign affiliates between 1961 and 1968, of about 13 per cent (see Multinational Corporations in World Development, op. cit., p. 14).

20. See Multinational Corporations in World Development, op. cit., p. 127 et seq.

21. See Business in Foreign Countries, United States Department of Commerce, Officebusiness Economics, Washington, 1960, p. 144, Table 55.

22. See J.W. Vaupel, J.P. Curhan, The Making of Multinational Enterprise, Boston, 1969, pp. V and 3. The enterprises mentioned were listed in Fortune's "500 Largest United States Industrial Corporations" for 1963, published in 1965.

23. See the current monthly reports of the Deutsche Bundesbank, vol. 17-24.

24. See Multinational Corporations in World Development, op. cit., p. 7.

25. Ibid., p. 7. According to a study by W.B. Reddaway (Effects of United Kingdom Direct Investment Overseas, Cambridge 1967) some 46 firms accounted for 71 per cent of manufacturing assets overseas in 1962 and 3 firms owned virtually all petroleum assets overseas.

26. See J.H. Dunning, The Multinational Enterprise: The Background, in: J.H. Dunning (ed.), The Multinational Enterprise, London, 1971, p. 20.

27. See Deutsche Bundesbank, Ausländische Beteiligung an Unternehmen in der Bundesrepublik, in: Monatsberichte der Deutschen Bundesbank, vol. 24 (1972), No. 1, p. 44.

28. See "Multinational Undertakings and Community Regulations", Communication from the Commission to the Council, presented on 8th November, 1973 Bulletin of the European Communities, Supplement 15/73.

29. Ibid., p. 12 et seq.

30. Ibid., p. 13.

31. See the Impact of Foreign Direct Investment in the United Kingdom, op. cit., p. 91.

32. Ibid., p. 92.

33. See United States Department of Commerce, Foreign Business Investments in the United States. A supplement to the Survey of Current Business, Washington, D.C. 1962, p. 5 et seq.

34. See G.Y. Bertin, Les investissements des firmes étrangères en France, Paris, 1962, p. 246.

35. As regards Brazil, e.g. see E.N. Baklanoff, Foreign Private Investment and Industrialisation in Brazil, in: E.N. Baklanoff, New Perspectives of Brazil, Nashville, 1966, for further data on Brazil and Mexico see R.S. Newfarmer, Structural Sources of Multinational Corporate Power in Recipient Economies, Draft Paper for CONOCYT Conference on Multinational Corporations, Queretaro, Mexico, March/April 1975, p. 17 et seq.

36. See among others J.H. Dunning: Multinational Enterprises, Market Structure, Economic Power and Industrial Policy, International Conference on International Economy and Competition Policy, Papers and Reports, Tokyo, September 1973 p. 191 ; R.E. Caves, International Corporations. The Industrial Economics of Foreign Investment Economica, Vol. 38 (1971), p. 1 et seq.

37. See, inter alia, United Nations, Multinational Corporations in World Development, New York, 1973 ; H. Krägenau, Umfang der multinationalen Investitionen, in: D. Kebschull, O.G. Mayer (ed.), Multinationale Unternehmen, Anfang oder Ende der Weltwirtschaft ? Frankfurt a.M., 1974, p. 15 et seq.

38. See in particular S. Hymer, The International Operations of National firms: A Study of Direct Investment, Dissertation MIT 1960 ; R. Vernon, International Investment and International Trade in the Product Cycle, Quarterly Journal of Economics, Vol. 80 (1966), p. 190 et seq.; C.P. Kindleberger, American Business Abroad, New Haven and London, 1969 ; S. Hymer, R. Rowthorn, Multinational Corporations and International Oligopoly: The Non-American Challenge, in: C.P. Kindleberger (ed.), The International Corporation, Cambridge/Mass. 1970, p. 57 et seq. R.E. Caves, International Corporations: The Industrial Economics of Foreign Investment, Economics, Vol. 28 (1971), p. 1 et seq.

39. For the most comprehensive study see H.J. Robinson, The Motivation and Flow of Private Foreign Investment, Menlo Park, 1961, p. 25, Table IX ; see also Implications of Multinational Firms for World Trade and Investment and for United States Trade and Labor, Report to the Committee on Finance of the United States Senate by its Subcommittee on International Trade, Washington, 1973, p. 108.

40. See, inter alia, C.P. Kindleberger, American Business Abroad, New Haven and London, 1969, p. 32 ; Steuer Report, op. cit., p. 10.

41. See, inter alia, S. Hymer, The Efficiency (Contradictions) of Multinational Corporations, The American Economic Review, Papers and Proceedings, Vol. LX (1970), p. 443.

42. Advantages of this kind are evidenced by the fact that foreign subsidiaries are typically less vertically integrated than their direct domestic competitors and that manufacturing operations of subsidiaries

are less integrated than the home production of the parent enterprise, see R.E. Caves, International Corpo rations: The Industrial Economics of Foreign Investment, op. cit. , p. 13 and the literature cited there.

43. Economic sectors with heavy product differentiation and a large proportion of foreign investmen capital are, inter alia, the food, drink and tobacco industry, detergents, the pharmaceutical industry, the automobile industry as well as electrical engineering.

44. See J.S. Bain, Industrial Organisation, New York, London and Sydney, 2nd ed., 1968, p. 260 e seq.

45. See C.P. Kindleberger, American Business Abroad, op. cit., p. 36.

46. See R.E. Caves, International Corporations: The Industrial Economics of Foreign Investment op. cit., p. 15.

47. See, inter alia, J.H. Dunning, Multinational Enterprises, Market Structure, Economic Power, and Industrial Policy, op. cit.; R.E. Caves, International Trade, International Investment, and Imperfect Mar kets, Special Papers in International Economics, No. 10, November 1974, p. 21 et seq.

48. See E. Heuss, Die Wettbewerbs- und Wachstumsproblematik des Oligopols, in: H.K. Schneider (ed.), Grundlagen der Wettbewerbspolitik, Schriften des Vereins für Socialpolitik, Neue Folge Bd. 48, Ber lin 1968, p. 50 et seq.

49. Cf. para. 44 et seq.

50. See, inter alia, J.N. Behrman, National Interests and the Multinational Enterprise, Englewood Cliffs/N.J., 1970, p. 43 et seq.

51. See, inter alia, R.E. Caves, International Trade, International Investment, and Imperfect Markets op. cit., p. 23 et seq. and the literature given there.

52. See, inter alia, R.M. Cyert, J.G. March, A Behavioural Theory of the Firm, Englewood Cliffs/N.J., 1963, pp. 36-38.

53. See H.G. Johnson, The efficiency and welfare implications of the international corporation, in C.P. Kindleberger (ed.), The International Corporation, Cambridge/Mass. and London, 1970, p. 40

54. The claim that multinationals do not use this possibility cannot be supported by the argument that in many cases they actually pay higher wages, since this does not take account of the fact that, as a rule, multinationals employ labour with above-average qualifications (see Steuer Report, op. cit., p. 99). See also "Wages and Working Conditions in Multinational Enterprises", International Labour Office, Geneva 1975.

55. See C.P. Kindleberger, American Business Abroad, op. cit., p. 64 et seq.

56. In this context, Murray speaks of an "internationalisation of cartelisation" (see R. Murray, Underdevelopment, International Firms, and the International Division of Labour in: Towards a New World Economy, Rotterdam, 1972, p. 228 et seq. ; see also S. Hymer, Direct Foreign Investment and the National Economic Interest, Yale University, Center Paper No. 108, New Haven, 1967).

57. See, inter alia, C.P. Kindleberger, The International Corporation, op. cit., inter alia p. 8 ; R.E. Caves, International Trade, International Investment, and Imperfect Markets, op. cit., 25.

58. See S. Hymer, R. Rowthorn, Multinational Corporation and International Oligopoly: The Non-American Challenge, in: C.P. Kindleberger (ed.), the International Corporation, op. cit., p. 57 et seq. United States enterprises' engagement in Europe, in turn, is justified by the authors who suggest that the posi tion of United States enterprises of the world market seemed to be threatened by the higher growth rates of European competitors.

59. Cf. J.H. Dunning, American Investments in British Manufacturing Industry, London, 1958, pp. 159-160.

60. Cf. J.N. Behrman, National Interests and the Multinational Enterprise, London, 1970, p. 21.

61. Cf. D.T. Brash, American Investment in Australian Industry, Cambridge/Mass. 1966, pp. 182-183.

62. Cf. R.E. Caves, Multinational Firms, Competition and Productivity in Host-Country Markets, Economica, Vol. 41 (1974), pp. 176-193.

63. Cf. Gervaise, Investissements étrangers, op. cit., p. 181.

64. Foreign Direct Investment in Canada, Ottawa, 1972.

65. Hogan, "British manufacturing subsidiaries in Australia and export franchises" ; paper presented to the Economic Society of Australia, New Zealand, New South Wales Branch, September 1965.

66. Special Report on Prices of Tractors and Combines in Canada and other Countries, Ottawa, 1969, p. 3.

67. Report by the Tariff Board, Photographic Equipment, Reference 147, Ottawa, 1974.

68. Kodak, Decision of the EC Commission of 30 th June, 1970, O.J. L.147/24 ; Pittsburg Corning Europe, Decision of the EC Commission of 23rd November, 1972, O.J. L.272/35.

69. See paras. 76 and 77 below.

70. Of the 21 enterprises participating in a rationalisation cartel for communication cables in Germany 11 were under the control of multinational firms.

71. Cf. Export Cartels, Report of the Committee of Experts on Restrictive Business Practices,OECD, Paris 1974.

72. Trade Practices in the Phosphorus Products and Sodium Chlorate Industries, Report of the Restrictive Trade Practices Commission of Canada, Ottawa, 1966, RTPC No. 41.

73. E.g. in the international Quinine Cartel, cf. "Prices of Quinine and Quinidine", Hearings before the Sub-Committee on Antitrust and Monopoly of the Committee of the Judiciary ; United States Senate, 89th Congress, 2nd Session (1966), 90th Congress, 1st Session (1967), Washington, D.C., United States Government Printing Office.

74. J.D. Gribbin, Restrictive Business Practices, Multinational Companies and Trade with Developing Countries, paper presented at the World Trade Institute Symposium « Antitrust Problems in the International Sphere", New York, 27-29th January, 1975, p. 8 and Table 9.

75. Gribbin op. cit. Table 9. Industrial concentration is measured by the percentage of sales made by the 5 largest companies within a product group. Source: Census of Production 1968.

76. Corresponding tables for other countries do not distinguish between cartels with or without multinational participation so that the figures contained in them are not representative of this study. See Export Cartels, OECD, Paris 1974, Annex II Japan, Annex III Netherlands, Table 2, Annex IV United Kingdom, Table 2, Annex V United States, Table 5.

77. In re Water-Tube Boilermaker's Agreement, Reports of Restrictive Practices Cases, Vol. I (1959), p. 285 et seq.

78. Die Kartellisierung in der Schwedischen Papier – und Pappeindustrie, Information der deutsch-schwedischen Handelskammer, Stockholm, February 1968, p. 16 et seq., UNCTAD Report, paras. 214-219.

79. Reported by the Federal Cartel Office for this study.

80. Report Concerning the Manufacture, Distribution and Sale of Drugs, Restrictive Trade Practices Commission, Ottawa 1963.

81. Hansard, unrevised, Ottawa, 12th February, 1968, pp. 6622-23. Similar findings were made in the Bristish Hoffmann-La Roche Case, see below para 76.

82. WEA-Fillipacchi Music S.A., Decision of the EEC Commission of 22nd December, 1972, J.O. No. L 303/52.

83. Cf. above para. 52 et seq.

84. Prices for tractors in Sweden are generally 10-15 per cent higher than in Denmark.

85. Published in the Series: "EEC Studies on Competition – Approximation of legislation" 1976 No. 26.

86. Report of the Monopolies Commission on the Supply of Chlordiazepoxide and Diazepam, H.M.S.O., 1973.

87. By a decision of the Netherlands Economic Minister of 4th April, 1974, the firms which had formerly supplied the independent wholesalers were ordered to resume supplies at the same reduced level they applied to their contractual dealers. The provisional order was rescinded on 18th December, 1974 when the wholesalers' group was again able to obtain sufficient petrol at a reasonable price.

88. Decision of the Berlin Court of Appeals of July 1974, "AGIP" WuW/E OLG 1499. Only due to the special circumstances of this case the Court held that there was no duty to supply.

89. Cases of such tying agreements have frequently been found in Denmark in the mineral oil sector ; individual cases have also become known in the Federal Republic of Germany.

90. Judgment of the European Court of Justice, of 15th July, 1972, O.J. No. C 130.

91. Judgment of the European Court of Justice, of 14th July, 1972, O.J. No. C 125.

92. Decision of the Commission of 21st December, 1974, J.O. L 343/19.

93. This agreement which also contained other provisions, was allowed by the French competition authorities.

94. Cf. Mergers and Competition Policy, Report of the Committee of Experts on Restrictive Business Practices, OECD, Paris, 1974, para. 110 et seq.

95. The 1972 figures also include service industry mergers which were not included in the figures from 1966 to 1971.

96. Cf. Mergers and Competition Policy, op. cit. para. 117 et seq., (figures for Canada subsequently updated).

97. E. Rosenbluth, The Relation between Foreign Control and Concentration in Canadian Industry, Canadian Journal of Economics February, 1970.

98. Cf. United Nations, Multinational Corporations in World Development, op. cit. p. 24 et seq. ; Commission of the European Communities, Multinational Undertakings and Community Regulations, op. cit. ; p. 12 ; Steuer Report op. cit., para. 5.35 ; F. Heidhues, Zur Theorie der Internationalen Kapitalbewegung, Tübingen 1969, p. 197.

99. Cf. J. Vaupel, J. Curhan, The World's Multinational Enterprises, Geneva 1974, P. 330 et seq.

100. Raymond Vernon, Multinational enterpises in developing countries : an analysis of national goals and national policies.

101. Decision of 9th December, 1971, O.J. No L7.

102. Judgment of the European Court of Justice of 21st February, 1973, O.J. L69.

103. Annual Reports on Competition Policy in Member countries, OECD, Paris, 1975, No. 2, para 229 et seq.

104. Cf. Mergers and Competition Policy, op. cit., para 141.

105. United States v. Monsanto Company, Farbenfabriken Bayer AG and Mobay Chemical Company CCH Trade Cases 1967, para 72,001

106. Silberston: International Patenting and Licensing and Competition Policy, Paper prepared for the Tokyo Conference, 1973, P. 7.

107. Centrafarm B.V. and Adriaan de Peijper v. Sterling Drug Inc. (1974-1976) ECR 1147.

108. OECD Council Recommendation concerning action against restrictive business practices relating to the use of patents and licences [C(73)238(Final) of 25th January, 1974] – See Annex III of the present report.

109. Taylor/Silberston: The Economic Impact of the Patent System, Cambridge 1973, p. 124 et seq.

110. Restrictive Business Practices relating to Patents and Licencess , Report by the Committee of Experts on Restrictive Business Practices, OECD, Paris, 1972, para. 34.

111. For further cases cf. Restrictive Business Practices relating to Patents and Licences, op. cit., Annex II, para. 110.

112. Taylor/Silberston: Economic Impact of Patents, op. cit. p. 125.

113. The cases of unreasonable restraints of trade consisted of one patent pool case and two cases involving quantity restrictions found in licensing contracts for television sets.

114. The number of contracts which received guidance does not coincide with the number of restrictions subject to administrative guidance, due to the fact that two or more items of a contract can be the object of a separate guidance.

74

115. Tätigkeitsbericht des Bundeskartellantes für das Jahr 1972, p. 63.

116. Tätigkeitsbericht des Bundeskartellamtes für das Jahr 1974, pp. 80 ff.

117. Cf. e.g. the U.S. Xerox Case, FTC News Summary No. 16/1975, 18th April, 1975.

118. Taylor/Silberston : Economic Impact of Patents, p. 158. Without distinguishing between national and multinational enterprises the authors found that cross-licensing agreements were present in 8 per cent of all licensing agreements in the chemical industry, in 5 per cent of all licensing agreements in mechanical engineering and in 20 per cent of all licensing agreements in electrical engineering in Great Britain.

119. Southern District of New York, Civ. 24-12, 30th July, 1952.

120. United States v. Fisons Limited et al. (23rd July, 1969, N. D. Ill.? Civ. No. 69 C 1530).

121. United States v. Bristol-Myers Co. et al. (19th March, 1970, D.D.C. Civ. No. 822-70).

122. United States v. Glaxo Group Limited and Imperial Chemical Industries Ltd. et al. (4th March, 1968) D.D.C. (Civ. No. 558-68).

123. United States v. Westinghouse Electric Corporation et al. (22nd April, 1970, N. D. Calif. , Civ. No. C 70–C852 – SAW).

124. Section 1 of the Sherman Act. The declaration of extraterritorial jurisdiction in this field is contained in the Clayton Act which defines the term "commerce" as including "commerce with foreign nations". Section 5 of the Federal Trade Commission Act refers to "unfair methods of competition in or affecting commerce". "Commerce" is defined in Section 4 of the Act to include "commerce... with foreign nations... or... between... any State... or foreign nation". Exercice of this extraterritorial jurisdiction by the United States Courts has produced a considerable volume of case law. For further details, see the OECD Guide to Legislation on Restrictive Business Practices, United States, Section 2, where this case law is set out in detail.

125. In Sweden, for example, the Act to Counteract Restraints of Competition in Business in Certain Instances states in Section 6: "Without the permission of His Majesty, negociation may not deal with effects arising outside Sweden from restraint of competition. Such permission may be granted only so far as it is required as a result of agreements with Foreign Powers."

126. For extensive treatment of this question, see the conclusions of Advocate General Mayras in the ICI/Commission case. (Case N° 48-69 – Reports of cases before the Court 1972-5, pp. 694 to 702).

127. See paragraph 121 and following.

128. In the explanatory memorandum to the bill the Government explicitly stated that concrete acts on Netherlands' territory must have taken place for the Act to be applied.

129. See Sections 6(1) and 36(3) of the Restrictive Trade Practices Act 1956.

130. See Section 5(1) and (2) of the Trade Practices Act 1974.

131. Section 98(2) of the Act of 1957 against Restraints of Competition.

132. Sections 4 and 40(1) of the Cartels Act.

133. Section 2 of the Monopolies Control Act.

134. Sections 1 and 2 of the Act against Restraints of Competition.

135. Sections 59 bis and 60 of the Decree of 30th June, 1945.

136. Section 5 of the Act of 1953.

137. Section 15 of the 1973 Act.

138. Restrictive Trade Practices Commission: Report on Shipping Conference Arrangements and Practices, Ottawa 1965, and also Rex v. Elliott (1905), 9 C.C.C. 505 (trial and appeal) and Regina v. Burrows et al. (1968) 54 C?P.R. 95.

139. Case concerning Nippon Yusen Kaisha and 5 other companies. Decision of 28th August, 1972.

140. Judgment of the Federal Court of 21st March, 1967, Hachette S.A. – Newspaper co-operative society ATF 93 11 192.

141. United States v. Aluminium Company of America [148 F. 2d. 416 (2nd Circuit 1945)].

142. Grosfillex/Fillistorf decision (O.J.E.C. N 58 of 9th April, 1964, p. 915 et 916/64) and Béguelin judgment of 25th November, 1971 (Court of Justice Law Reports Vol. 1971-6, p. 949). It should also be recalled that Article 85 of the EEC Treaty prohibits as incompatible with the common market, without distinction of nationality or domicile, "all *agreements between undertakings...* which have as their object or *effect* the prevention, restriction or distortion of *competition within the common market...*"

143. "It is the exercise in Belgium of the predominant influence (of the cartel or dominant position) which serves as the connecting link with Belgian legislation. The nationality of those holding the economic power, the place where the cartel was formed or the seat of the cartel's central organs have no relevance in this respect." (Van Reepinghen and Waelbroeck: quoted by Advocate General Henri Mayras in Case N° 48/69 ICI v. Commission, op. cit., p. 695).

144. Court of Justice Law Reports, op. cit., p. 699.

145. 148 F. 2d 416 (2d. Cir. 1945).

146. See in this connection the Antitrust Ombudsman v. Dubbman AB ; the Antitrust Ombudsman v. G-K-N Stenman AB and Bulten Kantal AB ; and the Antitrust Ombudsman v. Swedish Flour Millers Federation (described in OECD Guide to Legislation on Restrictive Business Practices, Sweden, Section 3., Case Nos. 28, 33 and 36).

147. See the judgment of the Federal Court of 21st March, 1967 (Hachette S.A. – Co-operative association of newspaper merchants) ; ATF 93 II 192.

148. Official Journal of the European Communities, N58 of 9th April, 1964, pp. 915-6/64.

149. Official Journal of the European Communities of 21/10/72, N°C 111/17.

150. Judgment of 25th November, 1971 (Court of Justice Law Reports 1971-6, p. 949).

151. Conclusions of Advocate General Henri Mayras, op. cit., p. 692 et seq.

152. See OECD Guide to Legislation on Restrictive Business Practices, EEC, Section 3.0, pp. 30-31.

153. Christiani and Nielsen case, O.J. N° L 165 of 5/7/69.

154. Judgments of the Court of Justice of 14/7/72 in case nos. 48/69, 49/69 and 51/69 to 57/69, European Court of Justice Law Reports, Vol. 18, 1972-5.

155. Judgments of the Court of Justice in case nos. 6 and 7/73, European Court of Justice Law Reports, Vol. 18, 1974-3.

156. 370 U.S. 690 (1962).

157. Docket N° 8778, decided 10th April, 1969.

158. Docket N° 8909.

159. CCH Trade Cases, par. 73,269 (S.D.N.Y. 1970).

160. Civ N° 822-70 (D.D.C.)

161. 1963 Trade Cas., par 70,600 (S.D.N.Y. 1963).

162. 100 F. Supp. 504 (S.D.N.Y. 1951).

163. Contacts jurisdiction means jurisdiction which may be based on the simple existence of business dealings.

164. In the Matter of the Grand Jury Subpoena Addressed to First National City Bank [396 F. 2d 897 (1968)].

165. It should also be mentioned that the OECD Industry Committee has a mandate to assemble statistical data on multinational enterprises, including the degree of penetration of multinational enterprises and the degree of concentration in the different industrial sectors.

166. In the United States, the Securities and Exchange Commission requires submission by all publicly owned companies, including foreign companies which sell stock or depository receipts in the United States, of extensive data concerning their businesses. The requirements include detailed figures on income, expenditures, profits, losses, investments, etc. This data is then made public in its entirety. The objective of such disclosure is to prevent fraud on investors in the reporting companies, but the information is also often useful as background for antitrust investigations. In most cases, however, the antitrust enforcement authorities must obtain substantial additional information from the companies themselves before institution of proceedings.

167. 13 F.R.D. 280 (D.D.C. 1952) (International Oil Cartel investigation).

168. See e.g. Order by United Kingdom Government to Beecham Group, Ltd. not to produce documents in response to a U.S. court order ; discussed in Antitrust and Trade Reg. Rep. N° 595 A-5 (9th January, 1973).

169. 396 F. 2d 897 (1968).

170. Ibid. at 899.

171. Ibid. at 902.

172. Ibid. at 903.

173. But see, In re Grand Jury Investigations of the Shipping Industry, 186 F. Supp. 298, 318 (D.D.C. 1960) where the District Court postponed an order for production, even though the foreign governments involved appeared not to protest production if the court so ordered, until the government exhausted all other possibilities for obtaining the needed information and could therefore demonstrate a need for the foreign documents.

174. 333 U.S. 795 (1948).

175. Ibid., at 818.

176. Ibid.

177. United States v. The Watchmakers of Switzerland Information Center, Inc., 133 F. Supp. 40, 45 (S.D.N.Y. 1955).   178. Hoffman Motors Corp. v. Alfa Romeo, 244 F. Supp. 70, 78 (S.D.N.Y. 1965).

179. 1968 Trade Cases 72,569 (D.D.C. 1968).

180. 68 Cr. 870 (S.D.N.Y. 1968), 70 Civ. 2079 (S.D.N.Y. 1970).

181. See footnote 163.

182. Civ. N791-69.

183. Civ. N68-141 W.

184. Judgment of 14th July, 1972, Case Nos. 52/69 and 53/69, Law Reports of the Court of Justice of the European Communities, Vol. 18.

185. ICI v. Commission, Case 48/69.

186. Judgment of 21st February, 1973 in case 6/72 (Reports of Cases Before The Court of Justice of the European Communities, 1973-2, pp. 241-242).

187. Case concerning Nippon Yusen Kaisha and 5 other companies. Decision of 28th August, 1972.

188. Berlin Court of Appeal Decision of 14th May, 1974, Cartel Section 24/74.

189. the possibility existing in the United States of leaving a case pending for many years if the foreign defendant refuses to appear in court is worth noting since this may also exert an influence on multinational enterprises to appear and, eventually, to comply with the decision taken.

190. Interamerican Refining Corp. v. Texaco Maracaibo, Inc. 307 F. Supp. 1291 (D. Del. 1970).

191. 285 F. Supp. 949 (S.D.N.Y. 1968).

192. 213 U.S. 347 (1909)

193. 331 F. Supp. 92 (C.D. Cal.1971), aff'd per curiam ; 461 F. 2d 1261 (9th Cir. 1972) cert denied, 409 U.S. 950 (1972) ; 274 U.S. 268 (1972).

194. 274 U.S. 268, 276 (1926)

195. See Continental Ore Company v. Union Carbide and Carbon Corp., 370 U.S. 690, 706-707 (1962) ; United States v. The Watchmakers of Switzerland Information Center, Inc., 1963 Trade Cas. 70,600 at 77,456-57 (S.D.N.Y. 1962) ; and the leading case, United States v. American Tobacco, 221 U.S. 106 (1911).

196. See however paragraphs 115 to 117 with regard to Canada.

197. Decision of the Commission of 30th June, 1970, O.J. NL 147 of 7th July, 1970, page 24.

198.   Case 15/74.   Decision of the Court of Justice of 31st October, 1974.

199.   Timken Roller Bearilg Co. v. United States, 83 F. Supp. 284 (N.D. Ohio 1949), upheld 341 U.S. 593, 598 (1950).

200.   See Annex IV, for example, for the OECD guidelines.

201.   The Delegate for Switzerland abstained.

202.   This Recommendation does not apply to Switzerland.

OECD SALES AGENTS
DÉPOSITAIRES DES PUBLICATIONS DE L'OCDE